OPEN SECRETS

Also from *Sydney Review of Books*

The Australian Face: Essays from the Sydney Review of Books
Second City: Essays from Western Sydney

OPEN SECRETS
ESSAYS ON THE WRITING LIFE

EDITED BY CATRIONA MENZIES-PIKE

First published 2022
by the Sydney Review of Books
from the Writing and Society Research Centre
at Western Sydney University

Locked Bag 1797
Penrith NSW 2751
www.sydneyreviewofbooks.com

Designed by Jenny Grigg
Typeset by Andrew Davies
in Tiempos Regular 9/15pt

Printed and bound by SOS Print + Media
Distributed in Australia by NewSouth Books

A catalogue record for this book is available from the National Library of Australia.

ISBN 978-0-6480621-6-5

9 8 7 6 5 4 3 2 1

Contents

Introduction

Catriona Menzies-Pike

The first myth about literary work in Australia is that writers don't actually do much of it. Debauched, unworldly, undeserving, lavished with more public money than they deserve – they enjoy a sinecure funded by taxpayers, for which privilege they are asked little in return. Read, write, lounge, scrounge. The second myth is that to be a writer is to have answered a divine call. If writing is a vocation, it's hardly work. Do what you love and you'll never work a day in your life. Bit rich to expect to get paid. Yet the reckless bon vivant and the worthy ascetic actually have few living counterparts in the corps of contemporary Australian literature. Most Australian writers don't get paid much for their work, not by publishers, not by readers, not by the government – which is hardly to say that they shouldn't.

So how – and why – does the work get done in a world that measures value in dollars and widgets and accords so little to literature? How are writers made? And how is writing made? These were the prompts the *Sydney Review of Books* issued to all kinds of writers, to the essayists and critics who are frequent contributors to the journal, and to poets, novelists and experimental writers. We sought essays that charted writing as a form of creative labour, and found ourselves with a large and eclectic set of works that deliver new insights into the creation of Australian literature.

How writers *get it done* is a staple of festival Q&As and magazine profiles. There are no precious morning rituals here, however, no magic tricks for aspiring writers, and little in the way of idealism. These essays document writing lives defined as much by procrastination, distraction and economic precarity as by desire and imagination, by aesthetic and intellectual commitments. Labour is at the heart of this collection: creative labour, yes, but also the day jobs, side gigs, and care work that make space for writing. The public funding available to Australian writers continues to contract, the prospects of healthy royalties from book publication are dim, and the gigs on which so many relied to pay bills, workshops, teaching, public events, have diminished in number. There's nothing in *Open Secrets* that conflicts with the regular reports from the Australian Society of Authors about the sinking financial returns of literary work. Many of the essays in this book, especially those authored during the Covid shutdowns in 2020 and 2021, are characterised by a discernible weariness.

Is it worth it? For readers, the work is the reward. As you'll discover, these essays are funny and intelligent and they quiver with joy and determination. For the writers gathered in *Open Secrets*, however, the true worth of literary work is a complex question that generates often contradictory answers. Writers may work alone in their rooms, but they are also creatures of the world, and each contributor to *Open Secrets* thinks in surprising ways about literature; they attest to forms of value beyond the economic, to the social, political and aesthetic dimensions of literary practice. This book offers portholes into the places where writing happens and portals to the new worlds and ways of living it might create. These essays bear witness to the resilience required to commit to the writing life – and to the vital transformative possibilities of literature, for writers, for readers and our culture.

Acts of Avoidance

Fiona Kelly McGregor

Saturday

It is midday on the first day of Lockdown and I'm at the desk. I have an essay and article to write while awaiting edits of my novel (working title *Iris 1)* from my publisher. Keen to clear the decks, I knock off some correspondence, check invoices then put through two loads of washing as rain is due. I tend to an orchid which has a bacterial infection.

I was supposed to be on holidays at my friends' olive farm in Wonnarua country. Reading in the morning, bit of work for the fellas in the afternoon. Cooking. Bliss. But I had to come home after three days to do a marking job. It took about sixty hours even though I could only log forty-seven according to the papers-per-hour of my allotted pay. The university IT system has changed since I last taught there and the new one took hours to figure out.

I earnt just over $1900. That's huge for me. If I earnt that much every week, I'd be in the second-highest income bracket. But I wouldn't be able to write.

I sign up for Mubi and find to my delight a ream of Kiarostami films. My housemate and I watch *The Wind Will Carry Us,* a sparse, meditative, absurd story set in a remote Kurdish village. The landscape looks incredible: stripes of yellow, ochre, green as though applied by a painting knife. The main character's jeep is constantly hooning in and out of these stripes as he heads uphill for phone reception to have frantic elliptical conversations about a dying woman we never see. I go to bed so stimulated I can't sleep.

Sunday

Awake at 6 a.m., I speed-read for my Zoom bookclub later that morning. It's a contemporary Australian novel that has won and been shortlisted for lots of prizes. Most people hate it though one of our best readers loves it. I don't say much: I'm still only halfway through. One member who works in public health reckons the lockdown will go for a while. 'We're going to have a big spike,' she says.

I spend the afternoon doing a Profit and Loss statement for Centrelink. I am keen to get off Jobseeker. I've been on it for a year as I haven't been able to get any part-time tutoring work. A lot of casuals lost work due to the drop in international students caused by Covid, but the real reason in Humanities departments is that the government cut funding. Enrolments are also down locally now an Arts degree costs around $30,000. The disastrous effects of Covid-19 on capitalism's casualised workforce are well known in hospitality, frontline health, border regulation, transport. The university teaching precariat is not at risk of contracting the virus, only of unemployment, poverty and depression.

I'm an autodidact, from choice rather than necessity. I'm not sure I believe in Creative Writing even though it's the only thing I'm qualified to teach apart from English as a Second Language. Covid and government funding cuts also stopped work in that sector. So in a way, being on Jobseeker is the government giving back what it took, but half as much, with bureaucratic surveillance.

I end the day with a perusal of the website of the artist I'm commissioned to write about. I'm excited about her work, we had an excellent interview. She's over seventy and there is so much material I can't get across it all. It's Sunday evening and I want a break.

Like almost every other artist and writer in this nation, I work around sixty hours a week. This doesn't include the hours of rumination off-desk, so to speak, necessary to creation. My basic routine for ten months was: Work on the novel Monday to Friday, 8/9 til 3/4 (I eat my meals at the desk). Then admin, chores, exercise. Saturdays are for ancillary work – pitches, reviews, articles, essays, commissions, applications. As I decided to apply for everything this year, the workload extended to nights.

I finished a draft of the novel at the end of May. I was so burnt out I did all the dumb things like leave my keys in the front door while I was out all day; wash blacks in hot water; start the wrong side of the HRT tray, ending up with a three-day migraine and night sweats. So I went on a holiday. For three days.

I dated a workaholic for a few months which was serendipitous. She's a scientist, also obligated to do grant applications. But she's an Associate Professor on a six-figure salary, the applications mostly done in working hours. There is nothing heroic about our white-collar workaholism; at worst it's a form of self-indulgence.

I get out for a walk. Leftovers for dinner. I had friends over on Lockdown Eve. I cooked rabbit with red wine and mushrooms: a feral shot by a friend on Gundungurra country. We sat around until after midnight when Lockdown officially began. Our fear of getting busted was only half jocular. The social contact of that night sustains me like the leftovers.

My housemate and I watch two episodes of *The Queen's Gambit*. I love the Jane Eyre orphanage, the giant chess games she watches on the ceiling as she lies in bed drugged. But how does she do that on downers? Are the green pills Ritalin?? I can't follow any of the games even though I can play chess. I like that too.

Monday

I sleep in, which discombobulates me. (I used to meditate every morning at six for an hour.) Then to the vet in a mask. I hate morning appointments. I'm a vampire who never goes out before three. Back home I look at the artist's photos and make notes. I write a few opening paragraphs, none of which work. Impostor Syndrome makes its obligatory entrance. *You didn't go to art school, you dropped out of uni, you've hardly read any theory.* The essay is for an art magazine. *You won't have enough citations!!*

A rejection in my inbox. My strike rate used to be one in ten, now it's about one in twenty. Could be reduced funding. Or age. Some applications have been under par and deservedly rejected. Others, like today's, are predictable. But one was unfair and I'm still mad about it. I fantasise about being important enough to snub the schmuck administrator one day. But I wouldn't know what she looks like and it would only give grist to her mill.

The important thing is to prevail.

In compensation, out of the blue I was asked to be Writer-in-Residence at Carriageworks; the outgoing was for visual art, I'm in for performance. I'm thrilled. But what will I write, now the venue is closed?

I am writing the art essay, and this one, to earn money. The external apron below my kitchen window is about to fall off; there are holes in my kitchen wall and it's twelve degrees down there in the morning. *Sydney Review of Books* pays well. This is what I've been paid by publications I've written for over the past years:

The Monthly – Print: $1 per word. Digital: $200 (flexible word count).

The Saturday Paper – 80c per word (profiles generally 2000 words, reviews 1100).
Sydney Review of Books – $750–1500 (dependent on length and essay type).
Artlink – 60c per word (usual length 1000–2000 words).
Meanjin – Digital: $200 (flexible word count; I haven't made it into print for years).
Runway – Digital: $200 (flexible word count).
Running Dog – Digital: $180 (flexible word count; now increased to $250).
Overland – Digital: $150 (flexible word count; I haven't made it into print for years).
Audrey Journal – Digital: $100–200 (around 1000 words).

These rates have remained the same since 2017, with *Overland* coming up from $120. The award nominated by Australian Society of Authors is 85c per word. It is worth noting that the list spans publications from private enterprises run by a multimillionaire, through to publications funded by universities, to young individuals and collectives scraping by on minimal funding. I don't know what the *Sydney Morning Herald* and *The Guardian* pay as they never reply to my emails.

Other jobs of the past year:

$200 for appearance on writers' festival panels. For a Sydney Writers Festival Gala Event I wrote a new piece which took a few days.
$500 for two appearances at Liveworks, a performance art festival. I wrote a new piece which took a few days.

Grant assessment – $750 for about 25 hours work.

Prize judging – $900 for reading 13 books, emailing and Zoom meetings.

I could live off this if I had two of these jobs per week. But that's impossible as the publications are mostly quarterly and essays and articles take about a week to write; besides which, I wouldn't have time to write my novel.

I am in the median earning bracket for Australian writers: $12,900 p.a., down from $20,000 p.a. ten years ago. I'll earn more this year, as I finish my novel, a once in a decade occurrence. Only the top 1–5% of Australian writers earn their living from writing. They are asked to work for free all the time – blurbing books, giving talks. I am too, and it's hard to say No because I am so desperate for work, and I risk offending people. Recently I was asked to appear for free at a seminar at a sandstone university. Three years ago, I appeared at a seminar at the same university. There was no fee offered then either but one of the other panellists was a media star, and his agent demanded $5000. The university suddenly found money; they bargained him down to $1500 and extended the fee to myself and the third panellist. But I'm not a media star and my agent this time advises me to say No; she is also often asked to appear for free by this university. 'They're the worst!'

I have published seven books, most selling only in the hundreds and difficult to contract. For my one bestseller, *Indelible Ink,* I have been on a royalty rate of 7.5% for more than five years due to a dodgy contract. The standard percentage is 10%; it should rise to 12% after a certain amount of sales have paid for editing and publicity. Rising royalties are advised by the ASA but they are rare and have to be fought for. From that 10% your agent takes 12–15%. My current agent deserves this and more.

I make dahl for dinner. I overcook it. Bad cooking for me often means good writing. Burnt pots mean the novel is humming along, especially if the fire alarm goes off and they have to be rushed outside pluming smoke then left to soak with bicarb of soda for days. I had a friend who used to bury his burnt pots in the backyard. But he's a lawyer.

The TV loses internet reception so I read. I race through the last hundred pages of the Australian novel and decide it's a brilliant idea – topical, apposite – but badly executed. I lie awake wondering if I'm harder on my fellow writers than my fellow artists. Wondering if I should write more novels and less essays. I'm longing for *Iris 1.*

Tuesday

Meditation, then a morning of procrastination which includes deciding to write this essay in order to avoid the art essay.

To avoid both of them, I fuck around on *Words with Friends* for nearly an hour. *WWF* is my digital addiction. I am *fiercely* competitive and only play high-scoring opponents. The endorphin rush is terrific. I've been known to punch the air when I score more than 100 for a word. I still remember Mary G from Wisconsin whom I was playing during the bushfires. She messaged me mid-game saying how sorry she was about the fires. Like a child given a lolly, I clustered to her, sending a teary rant about funding cuts to environmental programs, our Prime Minister being a climate-change denier almost as bad as Trump, but a right-wing Christian to boot, etc., etc. A gelid silence descended across the sixteen-hour time difference. I woke next morning in my smoke-filled house to a message from Mary G: *Well, the troops have been dispatched to Iraq, and the firefighters from California to Australia. I will pray for you.* It jolted me out of bed like a cattle prod. Then, Mary beat me. I was furious. I rematched. With cool precision, my extravagant vocabulary, a lot of luck and a pinch of cheating, I beat her. Then I beat her again, taking my tally to 5/4. I shouted and jumped for joy. Then I blocked her.

Fair to say, it has become a standard procedure of mine to block anyone I've won a majority against. It isn't spite, it's only to reduce my addiction, like deleting the dealer's number. But in *Words with Friends* there is a dealer on every corner. An opponent I know personally once posted his bedside reading on Facebook, including a cheater's book of words for *Scrabble*. So, I began to cheat against him. You know who you are.

It occurs to me that my entire working life has been made up of Acts of Avoidance. Performance art was done for years to avoid writing. *Indelible Ink* was written to avoid *Iris 1. Strange Museums* was written to avoid *Indelible ink,* as was *A Novel Idea. Buried not Dead* was written partly to avoid *Iris 1.*

Another marking job is offered. A 25,000 word Masters assignment for which I have to write a 2–4 page report. $274. The pay looks low but it's the award. I accept immediately.

I see the line-up for a writers' festival I've never been invited to and seethe with jealousy. Then shame. I read a terrific essay by Tristen Harwood, a young Indigenous critic and feel inspired. I create an Instagram post about a local performance I recently admired.

I work on the essay for about five hours and crack it. Then a long walk through Surry Hills, listening to Namila Benson interview

Sudanese-Australian Atong Atem, whose photographs I saw years ago at Customs House. Bedroom self-portraits in sci-fi dress-ups and fluoro make-up; photos of teenage friends. They return to me in all their wondrous highly coloured subversion as I walk through the drizzly early evening darkness. I am filled with love for my art community. All across this continent are diligent, talented, politically astute artists. Most struggle to make a living. This is why I write about them; this is why I used to make performance. Out of love.

Which doesn't mean you can ask me to work for free.

The TV still isn't working. I fuck around on my phone, deleting and merging contacts. I hover over an old client's number, then leave it. I read a couple of essays by Leslie Jamison, then Sontag's penetrating take on Diane Arbus in *On Photography,* then thirty pages of poems by Joseph Brodsky. I sleep the deep sleep of the well-nourished.

Wednesday

I am writing this essay out of frustration that few people understand the daily working lives of artists and writers and persist in dreamily thinking that our jobs are all dreamy thinking. It isn't their fault: government policies erase or trivialise us. Australia's mainstream media remains decades behind, foregrounding artists such as van Gogh and Marilyn Monroe. And can somebody do a search on how often *Spectrum* has featured Brett Whitely or Richard Neville in 1970s London as emblematic of bohemia? This is why, when we are on holiday, we always meet people whose eyes glaze over. The actor will get: Are you going to Hollywood? The artist: A painter! My mother likes painting. The musician: Are you a rock star? The writer: I'd write a novel if I had the time. All of us get: Would I have heard of you?

Removing our quotidian toil from public discourse entrenches elitism; the only visible thing is the end product, collapsed onto celebrity by hasty media. Lack of funding inflates prices, further reducing cultural access. But no artist who lasts into their forties is driven by delusions of fame: we just want to work.

Is this why it's so hard to get a holiday? Barthes's infamous claim that writing was as involuntary as shitting and holidays an invention of the bourgeoisie, compels me. Which takes us back to ...*If only I had the time.*

I read Cherine Fahd's monograph *Apókryphos,* with vignettes written by the artist and Daniel Mudie Cunningham. Inspired, I work all afternoon on the art essay. The body is down. I'm happy.

With spooky coincidence, my old client texts to see if I'm still working. I text back: Of course. See you after Lockdown! It's a fisting session. I was always good at that as my hands are long and slim. He's a sweet man, dribbly bum, small dick, gave me a beautiful corset. Bless. It's been years since I did a session. I ring a colleague to check the rates.

$350–450 depending on the content, and your experience. Not much of a wage rise since the height of my BDSM career twenty years ago. I was taught by old-school Mistresses, as we were called then. Clients were barely allowed to touch you. Rates were hourly, but it wasn't 'a clock-watching hour'. For twice as much money, we worked as submissives which was when clients got to fuck you. At $1000 per hour, caning sessions as a submissive were the best, but rare. Take your lover to a posh restaurant, gaze into her eyes, your arse cheeks pleasantly warm.

There was a famous BDSM establishment nicknamed Salon Shitty's because the Mistresses let clients fuck them. They also dropped their prices in the morning. It was one of the reasons the arse fell out of the industry. Later, my research for *Iris 1*, which is set in the 1930s, revealed that historically, kinky sex work often wove domination with getting fucked. My colleague tells me there is now another type of session called the Kinky Girlfriend experience, which I'm guessing is this and I'm glad it's a separate category. Better than letting them fuck you when you're Domming.

Nevertheless, once I subtract dungeon hire and calculate the time getting there, getting ready and cleaning up, it's not good pay and reminds me why I decided late in life to get some post-grad qualifications to teach. But I like to keep my hand in, so to speak.

By evening my back is sore from nine hours at the desk. I lie on the living-room floor groaning at the news. Covid ripping through Indonesia and India, the almighty vaccine fuck-up; $660 million for car parks, $125 million for live music, the thugs who rule us fortressing the country, when it isn't even theirs. What a pack of deadshits. Australia has become so protected, privileged, naïve, sterile, timid. Has it always been?

I want to stay on the floor and drink whiskey but I force myself out for a walk. I feel so lucky. I'm over fifty and healthy. My novel is contracted, I currently don't have caring responsibilities. I own a fucking house. Am I doing the right thing with all these resources? I wonder, as I do every day of my life.

I wake at 4 a.m. again. Will I lose gigs like I did last year? Sales? All the sex workers out of work, never mentioned because they're considered unworthy. The planet roils and seethes. I have to get this work done while I still can.

Thursday

I tie up the loose ends on the art essay. I suddenly feel flat about it but it's the best I can do. I have two pages of notes I couldn't include. I want to write more about her; I also feel inadequate to the task.

I Zoom two friends in México. One just had Covid despite the Johnson vaccination which she had to travel to the USA to get; she suffered only a few days fever and fatigue despite her asthma. The other is a doctor who didn't work for a year as the lack of PPE made it too dangerous. Now she is in Cancun, examining prison inmates to assess torture allegations. A third who had Covid last year, recently posted videos of a party: I goggle at the crowded dance floor. The music is fantastic. Later, this friend will tell me a lot of people got infected after the June party season, but not her, probably due to her antibodies.

My old cat climbs onto my lap and looks up at me with her huge emerald green eyes. Her purr vibrates through my body; oxytocin flows between us, quenching me.

On *Words with Friends*, I beat Alan S, whose profile shows a dapper young black man in the UK. My tally against him is now 12/11 so I block him. Sorry Alan, it's not personal. I start a game with my most formidable opponent Peggy, whose avatar is a pelican (I'm a king parrot). Peggy has the strongest crack on the block. By evening I'm edging ahead. With only one move left, she can't catch me now.

I go for a long walk with an artist friend who was due in Melbourne for a major exhibition of her work two days ago. She says she's handling it but I can tell she's upset. In contrast to my regularity, she worked a fifteen-hour day then a nothing day. The empty streets have lost their eerie allure and now just feel sad. She wears a mask the entire time.

The Queen's Gambit starts to lose me with the boozing. It feels like a man's version of a woman: the vision mostly surface, the mind and heart binaries, the strength of the former occluding the latter because smart women are freakishly cold. Another B-grade Netflix series.

I read another thirty pages of Joseph Brodsky. It's too stuffy. I will put the book on my front wall for the street faeries. He won the Nobel Prize for it.

Friday

As soon as I wake I open *Words with Friends* and find Peggy the Pelican has ended the game with ENHANCE over two triple-word tiles, scoring more than 100 points and totally wiping me out. I stumble out of bed bewildered.

I polish then file the art essay and send a copy to the artist for corrections. I do some work on this essay. Then on a third essay. I'm on fire, I'm delirious, it's a compulsion addiction vocation, I'm a hyperactive workaholic in Lockdown. I know this bout of anxious overwork will only result in burnout. I need to stop writing and do more reading. I walk up to Gleebooks to buy *A House for Mr Biswas* and some Ann Carson.

We finish watching *The Queen's Gambit* and I remain disappointed. More mid-twentieth century style for the furniture lovers. What orphanage in segregated 1950s USA could foster this mixed-race friendship? Was the actor cast black while the original character in the 1983 novel was white, as happened in the adaptation of *The Handmaid's Tale?* It feels more like a palliation than repudiation of racism, our leading lady of course hip to the jive. The incidents of sexism are little hurdles to be skipped over with barely a ruffle of her couture skirts, rather than the impassable roadblocks of the time. Then, a nice gay character to tick that last box. But it's had millions of viewers, *intelligent* viewers. It makes me think of the importance of not lying about history, not compromising for commercial gain, but also –

What can I get away with?

July 2021

Attachment Theory

Justin Clemens

Just as I'm reading A1's email inviting me to write for the *Sydney Review of Books*'s 'Writers at Work' series, another email pings in from B1, cc'd to M1, which is inviting me to invite B2 to co-write something for B1 and M1 on artists' writing, so I interrupt my reading of A1's mail to read B1's, which I then pretty much immediately forward to B2 in order to defer any decision to her, whereupon, having at least briefly evaded the taking-on of responsibility in the guise of its opposite, I return to A1's mail to try to think about whether I will have the time to actually write something about writing to write back to A1, when T1, with whom I am nominally writing a book about B3, sends me his completed chapter, simultaneously reminding me that I am lagging behind on my own delivery of a part-chapter, which, to do properly, means that I would physically have had to go to the Law Library to pick up a book on ancient near-Eastern practices of taxation and sacrifice – are the two ever fully separable? – and which I have also been avoiding out of a mild sense of fear and confusion, that is, at actually going to a specialist library to which I have (humiliatingly) never been before (though it is a mere ten-minute walk down the road) and attempting to negotiate an unfamiliar and potentially minatory space, let alone carefully reading through a technical treatise on a topic that, despite self-evidently being of supreme interest at once historical and contemporary, both generally and in particular, may take an amount of time and effort that will further retard my already very *en-retarded* schedule. Yet although T1's email thus inspires further panic, it at least impels me to read his attachment – reading not only as necessary prolegomenon to writing but perhaps more opportunistically as further alibi for procrastination – which turns out to be characteristically magisterial, at once 'clearly and accessibly written' as they say on the packet, if bulging with 'extraordinary and little-known' (ditto) details about the prehistory of the term *terra nullius*, and making an argument that seems never to have been made before about this foundational – or, rather, *anti*-foundational – doctrine of Australian colonial settlement, thereby throwing me immediately into a funk of metastatic ambivalence, i.e., terror and admiration if without any accompanying catharsis, whether you translate this supremely equivocal Aristotelian term as 'purgation' or 'purification'. My anxiety, fortuitously or not, is then immediately interrupted again – a request from M2 to contribute a short essay to a collection on the theme of *cryptocurrency* – which straightaway makes me think of P1's dictum that Australian politicians' universal enthusiasm for 'smart cities', that is, total surveillance sites in which you will immediately receive a text message from the government telling you *that your account has been docked for speeding while you are still engaged in the aforementioned act of speeding*, is an irremediably slavish enthusiasm for *factories of inhumanity*, which, naturally, only retriggers my anxiety, though now with a nominally different cause. The anxiety impels me to at once return to my half-finished powerpoint slide for an upcoming symposium on 'Disruptions of the Digital: Privacy, Civics, Democracy' – doesn't that just roll off the tongue? – with P1, I1, J1, K1, M3, N1, N2, R1 and T2, at which I intend to speak about the current *expropriation of the means of communication* by contemporary digital media, and which relies heavily on Hannah

Arendt's reflections in *On Violence* that: *No government exclusively based on the means of violence has ever existed. Even the totalitarian ruler, whose chief instrument of rule is torture, needs a power base – the secret police and its net of informers. Only the development of robot soldiers, which... would eliminate the human factor completely and, conceivably, permit one man with a push button to destroy whomever he pleased, could change this fundamental ascendency of power over violence. Even the most despotic domination we know of, the rule of master over slaves, who always outnumbered him, did not rest on superior means of coercion as such, but on a superior organization of power – that is, on the organized solidarity of the masters.* This declaration has since been rendered even more terrifying or at least more concrete given that, in the time elapsed between the first publication of Arendt's essay and the present, the uncanny techbros of Silicon Valley (and many other non-places too of course) have spent their days and nights essaying to perfect, first, the *internet of informers* that mercilessly tracks every thumb-swipe and finger-jab, from the quote-unquote *smartphones* we carry everywhere with us and which we cannot help 'gazing lovingly at and fondling' (as they say in the classics) even while driving on the freeway or in peak-hour inner-urban traffic, to the drones and surveillance cameras every moment tracking every fraction of the ground and the air, and, second, a regime of *robot soldiers* able to be deployed at an instant's notice anywhere on earth or in ether, all accompanied by an unprecedentedly vast and immersive media barrage of bad-faith boosterism and totalitarian jingoism dissimulating itself as libertarian emancipation. To cite P1 again, what ya gonna do when you're *deplatformed* by your own refrigerator? In a world of networked smartobjects, the 'internet of things', it won't do you any good to get another one cos the things are getting together and talking amongst themselves. And what are all the bright young smartobjects talking about these days? Whether you deserve to continue to enjoy the fruits of their labours; in a word, whether you should be *cancelled*. I guess I feel more people should feel the force of Sigmund Freud's insight in *Totem and Taboo* that 'emancipation from one renunciation is made up for by the imposition of another one elsewhere', that there's not only no escaping a repression of one's own, but also no escaping the malaise in civilisation because civilisation is itself constitutionally such malaise. What in any case would be the benefit in doing so? As Freud himself allegedly remarked to his daughter Anna when she told him how much money the SS had stolen when they searched the Freud family home in 1930s Vienna – 'they make even more from a house call than I do!' – the recollection of which anecdote triggers another spasm of half-forgotten obligations, for instance that I also have agreed (why?!) to write an endorsement for a scholarly collection on comedy edited by M4 & M5 that was – is? will be? – so interesting that I read it through in its entirety, an act that I believe to be almost never truly accomplished in academic circles, which, in the terms in which the nineteenth-century German philosopher Friedrich Nietzsche condemned the eminent philologists of his own times, usually means one *trundles* two or three hundred books a day without *reading* a single one, but then found I had to write and rewrite my enthusiasm down because the more truly I tried to convey my response the more my little blurb sounded like the breathless imbecility of an advertising algorithm, making it inappropriate for purpose unless I simulated a critical restraint I didn't feel. Yet that was hardly the end of the divagations and prevarications. Should a blurb for an academic collection on comedy be funny? 'Under the mask of humour,' says Gershon Legman, 'all men are enemies.' Probably not then. No sooner have I belatedly emailed the amended blurb, however, that I recall that L1 and I have to complete a grant application by Friday, so I email her before panicking that she may not receive the email in time so text her mobile phone for good measure, but, before receiving any reply from her, start to read the emails I have gotten in the forty-five seconds or so since sending my unfunny comedy blurb, among which is an automated email listing a set of emails that the email system itself has automatically blocked, including several to do with a seriously brief book by the French philosopher Alain Badiou that A2 and I have been translating that now bears the English title *The Pornographic Age*, which is likely what set the algorithm's bells ringing or moral senses twitching, so that it prevented the delivery of these emails, while, in a parody of prurience, somewhat tardily informing me of its own censorial actions. I then attempt to unblock the blocked emails which, it turns out, come with attached sets of proofs marked HIGH PRIORITY as, due to outsourced publishing deadlines, the expected turnaround is prohibitively tight, deadlines that, for better or for worse, I and A2 have conclusively missed, but which we would probably not have met anyway for a variety of reasons, not least justifiable irritation at being given so little time to check the proofs, an irritation that is often – although not in this case – ratcheted up even further by the scant resources most often given to external readers in such situations due to the corporate late-capitalist drive to *do ever more with ever less*, a drive whose vicissitudes could presumably be graphically depicted so that the impending moment at which one will have to accomplish infinite work with zero resources can be definitively identified. I then email A2 to propose a further delay, wondering if there will ever come a time when data anthologists of the future will come to the point of assembling works such as *The Collected Emails of Mark Zuckerberg and Jeff Bezos* in 571-volume Martian leather-bound sets, before realising this is exactly the role performed today by people like Julian Assange (sans the leather binding, obviously). In any case, any such epistolary exchange, whether real or fantasmatic, will undoubtedly share not even a shred of literary style with the great exemplars in the field: Aphra Behn's monumental *Love-Letters Between a Noble-Man and His Sister*, for instance. If, as Marshall McLuhan put it, the medium is the message, the medium that is email incarnates the contemporary crush for control over communication. People like to crap on a lot about free speech these days, but if you're using email at all, it really isn't free, it isn't private, and it isn't yours. My friend P2 who has now somehow made it as middle-aged middle-manager in a rapacious deracinated multinational corporation has described the *dashboard* that gives him access to his entire team's emails, complete with the merciless stats of who is online when and where sending what to whom. Emailing throughout the night? Good! Potentially taking 4 or 5 hours of sleep? Not good! At this point, my computer – really, the institution's computer – automatically logs me out of the system for security reasons, requesting that I enter my password. As my ten-year-old daughter said the other night while we were trying to *legally* download a movie – which took at least twenty irritating minutes of authorising security details and attempting to remember ancient passwords – in order to pay $4.99

for forty-eight hours' worth of access to something we could have more easily acquired for free through a pirate site, 'That's a lot of typing, Daddy.' If anybody had proposed to me as late as 1999 that most people in Australia would spend most of their days in front of a crazy variety of screens re-entering more and more recondite passwords while desperately trying to regain contact with some kind of responsible agent, I may plausibly have dismissed them as unduly pessimistic. After two decades of digital disruption, however, dystopian SF pessimism has become dreary quotidian actuality. A friend R1 recently spent her afternoon in a large office – to which she had gone in person as it had proven impossible to receive satisfaction online or on the phone – being referred from one administrator to another until, at the end of the day, she was referred to the very administrator with whom she began. Kafkaesque, yes, but R1 was not content to conclude by invoking this easy adjective. 'Look,' she said to me, 'everybody there is either new or in a new position that has been created by continuous restructuring of the organisation. As a result, nobody knows what exactly it is that they have to do, having not had the time nor training to be across the incredibly complex and indeed inconsistent and constantly mutating organisational processes. If they tell me something incorrect, then they are at risk of losing their job; they cannot say for sure whether what they tell me is correct or not; so it's vital that they help me by passing me onto somebody else who may be able to give the right answer; but since everybody is in this position, there is absolutely nobody left who can do this. Therefore in order to keep their job, it is necessary that they don't do their job.' This is civilisation perfected as an absolute deadlock. As Freud writes in 1937 to Princess Marie Bonaparte,

'I have an advertisement floating about in my head which I consider the boldest and most successful piece of American publicity: "Why live, if you can be buried for ten dollars?"' Good question. As the English psychoanalyst Hanna Segal answers, thinking of Cormac McCarthy's *The Road*: 'keep a little fire burning, however small, however hidden'. Just don't do it on email.

Award Rate

Laura Elizabeth Woollett

The morning I may win a life-changing amount of money, I try to look worthy of it. My new dress hangs, tags intact, as I watch the clock in my Park Hyatt bathrobe. Ten minutes pass. I send a Facebook message. No reply. I've already deposited $100. If I'm being ghosted, I only have myself to blame. Starving artists shouldn't waste money on professional hair and make-up. Twenty-nine-year-old women should know how to apply foundation.

A knock.

'What's the event?' the HMUA asks, laying out her kit in the smarting Canberra sunshine.

'An awards ceremony. For books.'

'I mostly do weddings,' she tells me. Last weekend, a wedding in the Blue Mountains, which paid well but came at a cost. Four hours' travel in each direction. Overpriced fuel. A cold caught from a bridesmaid. Straightening my hair, she resolves to cancel tomorrow's client. Better that than get sicker, infect her children, lose a whole week tending to runny noses. 'Sometimes the money doesn't seem worth it.'

I hum in sympathy, inhaling the expensive scorch of my hair.

'How old are you?' she asks, out of nowhere. When I answer, it's her turn to hum. 'You have a little grey coming through. I got mine early, too.'

—

I've never had a full-time job. I used to tell myself that this was a lifestyle choice; that the flexibility was worth the insecurity; that nine to five, five days a week would kill my creativity. Truthfully, I've never had an offer. Interviewing for full-time positions – data-entry, marketing assistant, medical receptionist – I was asked about my Creative Writing degree. I was asked about career aspirations. 'To live and write,' was my answer. Not a good answer.

—

Late in 2013, my year of Centrelink appointments, I'm offered a trial at a 24-hour flower shop. The manager sends me home with ten pages of workplace rules, which I read with mounting incredulity. *DO NOT OVER-WATER FLOWERS OR YOUR PAY WILL BE CUT. DO NOT LET FLOWERS DRY OUT IN THE SUN OR YOUR PAY WILL BE CUT. DO NOT MOVE FLOWERS FROM THE BACK FRIDGE OR YOUR PAY WILL BE CUT.* I don't show up for the trial.

In January, a woman rings and fires off a bunch of words: *CV, Gumtree, mystery shopping, 'writer'?*

I confirm, yes, I am a writer.

'That's good.' She laughs: a wheezy smoker's laugh, like old pipes heating up. 'We could use you.'

The flower shop, it turns out, was a drug front. I feel vindicated when the news breaks, but also a sting of disappointment. Imagine the stories.

—

Parliament House stands on stolen land in Ngunnawal, Ngunawal and Ngambri country. If anyone needs reminding, the Aboriginal Tent Embassy is one kilometre down the road, established as a site of protest in 1972 in front of what was then Parliament House. Lining up for security clearance, I'm unsure what to do with this knowledge, except add it to the cumulative discomfort. Half an hour earlier, I swallowed four dollhouse-pink beta-blockers, but my heart hasn't noticed. My blood, pumping through my veins, feels corrosive as battery acid.

After passing through security, I make my husband photograph me in the Mural Hall. We proceed to the morning tea. There are platters of macarons, fruit tarts, but I know a single bite will turn to nervous diarrhoea within five minutes. What was it Richard Flanagan said, when he won this award back in 2014? *Money is like shit. Pile it up and it stinks.*

My purse vibrates; my agent wishing me luck. I delay replying, not wanting to seem desperate, then forget altogether. Noticing a wall filled with framed pictures of middle-aged white men, my husband and I play at finding the most ghoulish. Then I check the time and think of clunky computers, bowls of alcohol wipes, the foamy padding of my headset, construction workers suspended in the milky-grey Melbourne sky.

'I wish I was at work,' I lament.

—

Mystery shopping doesn't have much to do with shopping, I soon learn. A minority of clients are Commercial – automakers, airlines, telecommunications. Then there's Utilities. Education. Finance. Councils. *Lots* of councils. Sometimes a special project comes along, like the public housing calls where we pretend we're disabled, mentally ill, mothers of seven children, fleeing domestic abuse, etc. We're encouraged to 'sound sad' for these calls. We're encouraged to 'sound angry' for complaint calls, such as the scenario that has us posing as homeowners, bristling over rumours of upcoming housing developments in our area. 'Scenario' is what we call the things we call about. 'Agent' is what we call the people we talk to. There are many turns a scenario can take, many variations of agent and agent behaviour, which is why they can use me, a 'writer'.

'Why wouldn't I just check their website?' I ask Dane, my training buddy, after bringing up a scenario requesting library opening hours.

'Because we hired you off Dumbtree.' He smirks. 'Or your internet's down. You can say that, if they ask. They won't, though. It's their job to be nice, no matter how dumb you sound.'

Dane has grey hair but a young face. He seems distinctly 'Melbourne', so I'm surprised to learn he's a Perth transplant like me, from my side of Perth. 'Ah, Single Mum Valley,' he muses, when I tell him my old suburb. 'No offence.'

I'm too busy multitasking to be offended: dialling, timing, listening, lining up my words. 'Have you checked the website?' the agent immediately asks.

After hanging up, I click through a series of 'YES/NO' ratings, then reach a box for 'commentary'. I type a few sentences, look back at Dane.

'That's enough,' he tells me. 'That's good.'

—

I'm on a Pacific Island with limited internet, on the home stretch of my new novel, when I get the news that the old novel has been shortlisted for the big award. Timing's a bitch. A year ago, when I wasn't writing, wasn't sure I'd write again, news like this would've been a lifeline. News like this might've reassured me that the labour was worth the burnout, might've prevented me from feeling personally injured by the high-octane, highly-Instagrammable success of a multi-award-winning peer. News like this might've made inspiration, when it struck again, seem less like a lightning-bolt I had to stab myself in the chest with, and more like something mundanely precious – a fresh green shoot, sun after rain.

Now, I'm on an island, drinking island wine, watching *The Bachelor*, with an avocado the size of a baby's head waiting to be cut open and a novel waiting to be written, and why this, why now, for fuck's sake? I started the year in ICU.

The Australian ***Prime Minister's Literary Awards*** *(PMLA)... are held annually and initially provided a tax-free prize of $100,000 in each category, making it Australia's richest literary award in total. In 2011, the prize money was split into $80,000 for each category winner and $5,000 for up to four short-listed entries. (Wikipedia)*

I send messages. I watch the final brunette fail to receive a rose. I agonise over how to announce the news, though not for as long as I normally would (island internet). I eventually opt for a bathroom-mirror underwear selfie, which I had no reason for posting before. I look good. Or maybe I just look conceited. The picture doesn't show the fang-like scar inside my thigh, from the femoral vas-cath I received dialysis through, back in March.

–

Beautiful commentary! Chantelle, the woman who hired me, emails throughout that first year, with examples of sentences I've written. *Just beautiful!*

Sometimes emails are sent to the wider team, containing my commentary and educational dot-points on what's good about it.

Sometimes I'm asked to proofread commentary written by my co-workers, especially if a project is important. Sometimes someone isn't sure if something is grammatical, or needs a synonym. Sometimes we mystery shop via email, and my emails, with their calculated spelling errors and TMIs, cause snorts of laughter.

I'm not the only creative in the call centre. Scrap paper is evidence of this: sketches, caricatures, lyrics. There are musicians among us. DJs. A filmmaker. A light-installation artist. A taxidermist. Some of us possess arts degrees. Others study social work, architecture, PhDs.

It's the best job I've ever had – which is to say, it isn't a factory, or a supermarket, or the bakery that underpaid me, or the juice bar that scolded me for not smiling enough, or the discount clothing store where I sold $20 jeans to boomer men. Which is to say, it pays more than $25/hr. But there's more I can say.

I can say: I write little stories every day, about agents and their actions and the implications of these actions. I can say: I lie every day. I'm a better liar. I'm a better listener. I'm better at noticing patterns of speech; hesitations, interruptions, assumptions, unspoken wants and needs. Before this job, my dialogue wasn't worth shit.

I can say: I talk to people every day. I like my workmates. I like the in-jokes about companies, agents at those companies, their mannerisms, improvements, backslides. I can say: sometimes something so ridiculous happens – like the agent who responds to an email enquiry with a video of himself preening and beaming, entreating our female alias to call him, please – I shake with silent laughter every time I think of it.

I can say: I know things. Bin days of streets I'll never live on. How to retrieve credit from a deceased family member's account.

How many pet chickens I can legally keep. I know the cost of houses across the country; not only to buy, but to live in – and while this knowledge may not be useful or reassuring, knowledge is power. I know the cost of living.

I can say: sure, there are bad days. Days when there's no conceivable way out. Days when I hate the sound of my own voice, and other people's. Days when I envy the construction workers in the opposite tower, because at least they're outside, doing something real and dangerous, rather than sitting at a desk trying not to break the fourth wall. I can say: on these days, a kind voice on the other end of the line means more than ever. Because even if she's calling me Anna, or Julia, or Marissa, it's the tone that matters, that reminds me I'm real.

—

The representative from the federal Department of Communications and the Arts has such a delightful email manner, I want to assess it and write beautiful commentary. Instead, I meet her in person. She's wearing the outfit she described in her email. She's excited; asks if I am, too.

'Well...nervous.' Actually, I'm pure fight-or-flight.

Some days, working on autopilot, I'll jolt awake inside my favourite toilet cubicle around midday, with no memory of how I got there or the events of the day so far. I try to switch into autopilot in the Parliament House bathroom, reading over the one-minute speech in my Notes app. All shortlistees were told to prepare a one-minute speech, *just in case*. The speech is probably fine. It thanks the people closest to me and the book. It says nothing about money or politics.

Money is like shit, Richard Flanagan said, before publicly donating his prize money to the Indigenous Literacy Foundation. I like this statement. But I also know Flanagan wasn't working in a call centre when he made it, was already a Booker Prize winner, probably living somewhere nicer than a unit with black mould and dripping fixtures. Which begs the question: at what point does the smell become offensive?

—

The week after I return from the island, training begins for a special project, which will provide us a month of full-time work – overtime, even – if we want it. We want it. We know, as casuals, that dry spells are beyond our control; a side-effect of client whims, managerial blunders, holidays, bushfires, pandemics. When it's raining, we reach for our buckets.

The client is a multinational automaker. We're mystery shopping every dealership in the country: metropolitan, provincial, rural; service and sales departments. Half of us can't drive. Our aliases, however, want to test-drive the latest hatchback, worth $37,000.

'But why are we replacing our 2012 hatchback, if we like it and it still works?' the light-installation artist asks.

'You're upgrading it.'

'But why?'

Chantelle, looking in on the training session, tells the project manager she'll have to explain the concept of upgrading to us 'left-wing hippies'. Falteringly, she does. Afterwards, the light-installation artist shakes her head and repeats, 'But...*why?*'

—

Scott Morrison's head looks as big and round IRL as it does on TV. He bobs into the auditorium, starts speaking, then bobs out again, on more pressing business. In his absence, Annabel Crabb, who's MCing, roasts him. She roasts him again when he returns. Grinning, he tells the audience his wife is a big fan of Crabb's books – her cookbooks.

I get a photo before he leaves again; post it to my Stories. *Omg ew*, my sister DMs.

He comes and goes so many times, I lose count. Announces the winner of Australian History, then bails. Meredith Lake sneaks back to her seat, which gives me hope that we can all just take the money and run. Then the Minister of Arts takes over and Lake is called back onstage. I don't absorb her speech, but it seems better than whatever's in my Notes app.

Within the next two months, the Department of Communications and the Arts will be slashed, merged into a conglomerate covering Transport, Infrastructure, and Regional Development. Within the next three months, the PM will piss off to Hawaii while the country burns. Within the next year, the Coalition will rule to double the cost of arts degrees, rendering them prohibitively expensive. I'm one of the lucky ones. Seven years after graduation, I'm a guest at Parliament House. I still don't know if I'll ever pay off my HECs debt.

–

I'm a lawyer. I'm an accountant. I'm a veterinarian. I'm a psychologist. I'm a bullshit artist, impersonating a person who buys $37,000 vehicles. 'Grief,' I say, when the agent asks what kind of psychology I specialise in. 'I'm a grief counsellor.'

As he clucks over my important job, I mark him 'YES' for 'personalised moment'.

I'm an author, in the running to win double what I earned last financial year, between writing and my day-job. Enough to afford *two* brand-new hatchbacks, and more. A new face. A mortgage. A mortgage on the island, with its baby-head avocadoes and limited internet. Or, donate it. Donate a portion, and keep the rest for myself, to live and write. Just that: *live and write*.

Days before the ceremony, I collapse on the carpet after work with my laptop-heavy backpack, groceries in a reusable bag. 'But, what if I win, and *can't* write?' I fret. 'What if I get so comfortable, I stop trying?'

My husband just shakes his head, says that's what they want us to think: that our labour has more value when it's uncompensated.

—

Before the Fiction category winner is announced, our book covers appear on-screen, accompanied by grave instrumental music and the judges' comments. It's a proud moment, theoretically. Physically, I'd rather be elsewhere. An hour forward in time, drinking free wine, reconciled to my fate, whatever it is. A few weeks back in time, happy on the island. Further back: hospital, cold with numbing cream, trying not to spew as the hard trapezium-shaped pillow jabs my stomach and the biopsy needle jabs my kidney. Even further: before hospital; before the lightning storm of can't-eat can't-sleep productivity that landed me there; before the year of not-writing; before the choice to write instead of doing something 'useful' – the kind of job where $80,000 is an annual salary expectation rather than a once-in-a-lifetime boon from a government that would prefer we didn't exist.

Thanks for the money, I imagine saying, then slipping offstage. Would that be too ungracious? Uninspiring? *Thanks for the money. It's a lot. I wish there was more to go around.*

It's a proud moment, theoretically. Physically, I want the earth to swallow me. When Crabb calls a name, not mine, the sinking of my heart doesn't register as disappointment. It's a return to normalcy.

—

The day after the ceremony, I'm rostered nine to seven: eight hours of regular mystery shopping, two of after-hours voicemails. When workmates ask about Canberra, I describe ScoMo's disappearing act, and nobody is surprised. Nobody mentions the money.

'How was Canberra?' Annie asks, coming in for her half-day at the 1 p.m. reshuffle. She's seven months pregnant, mostly on half-days.

'Alright.' I shrug. 'I didn't win.'

'Bummer.'

I don't know why I say it: vanity, misery, a desire to break from routine? 'Yeah. I'm a bit sad. It was a lot of money.'

'Yeah?'

'$80,000.'

'Wow, okay.' Annie laughs. 'I'd be sad, too.'

I watch her sterilise her headset. Failing to do so can cause colds, breakouts of jawline acne. 'It's not so bad,' I say. 'I still get $5000. All the shortlistees do.'

'Well, *that's* nice. What're you spending it on?'

'Bali for my 30th, probably.'

'Nice.'

I smile and slip my headset back on, slip back into character.

The sky behind the opposite towers is an inorganic, starless black when Chantelle shuffles up to my desk in the last half-hour of my shift. 'How're the voicemails going?'

'I can't get through.' I grimace. 'The agents keep picking up.'

'Tell me about it. Eva was here till eight the other night and didn't get any.'

'Shit.'

'Which is my way of saying, you're *welcome* to stay longer.'

'Oh. How long?'

She wheezes a laugh. 'How desperate are you?'

I shrug, smile.

'I'll be here for a while, anyway.'

I wonder why, when she's not paid by the hour, then figure it's probably for the same reason I write on my lunchbreaks, the same reason the agents won't let my calls go to voicemail. If you're not working overtime, you're not working hard enough.

'__ Sales Department, __ speaking. HowcanIhelpyou?'

I text my husband. Check Instagram; stray likes still sprouting up for yesterday's post, sprawled out on Parliament lawn with a bladder full of free wine. Dial again.

'Nice work.' Chantelle picks up her bag at 7.30. 'Don't forget to lock up.'

Twelve hours have passed since my alarm went off. I'll have to go to bed in the next four hours if I want eight hours' sleep. It takes thirty minutes to tram home; ten to earn my tram fare. Walking is free and good exercise, but will take over an hour.

'__ Sales Department, __ speaking. HowcanIhelpyou?'

7.52: I'm wavery, neon, a screen stared at too long. I can keep staring, for the money.

'__ Sales Department, __ speaking. HowcanIhelpyou?'

But sometimes the money doesn't seem worth it.

Secret Poems

Elena Gomez

I tried to write a poem about my writing practice and it was unsatisfying. My poems and my writing practice sit in different parts of my body. That is, there's a gut level thirst for writing poems, but it's my limbs and organs where the practice is embodied, where my poetry becomes embedded. I'm never 'inspired' to write. It's more a compulsion. In the grimmest terms, it's a disciplinary practice required for a restless body and mind. Someone once told me I possess an unfortunate mix of tendencies towards Protestant work ethic and Catholic guilt. This is a severe summary of my psychic energy; it's not something I should brag about. But I feel a sick sort of pride in it.

—

In Marilynne Robinson's *Home*, the main character Glory remembers how, as a child, she confused the words 'secret' and 'sacred'. It struck me how it was not a mere phonetic similarity these words shared (probably Robinson's intention), but that part of an object or ritual being sacred is indeed its mystery; its secrecy. Sacred is a historically common perception of poetry. Its practice is secretive.

Secretive could describe how it felt when I became a poet and I couldn't figure out how others wrote poetry. My poems were scrappy and not very artful, while the poetry of others reverberated in my body. But there is also Fred Moten's sense of the relation between the poem and the secret as always both collective and political: '[p]oetry enacts and tells the open secret'. In an effort to unmask conditions of being (in particular gendered and classed conditions), I began reading lots of Silvia Federici. I read Marx too (Karl, but also Eleanor). Anne Boyer and Alice Notley. I was brazen and read and listened to poets and thought 'I can do that' while simultaneously clutched by fear, thinking 'I can't do that'. I don't think I fall into the South Asian cliché of disappointing my parents for pursuing the arts, but that was the narrative I had for myself at the time (one reason I don't trust or write narrative). Trying poetry, having already embarked on a career in publishing, felt like an extension of the disappointment I imagined I bore.

I never found out exactly what the other poets did when they wrote, but I emphatically turned to the form anyway. Reading poetry seriously for the first time felt secret – sacred – to me. Poems are immortal. They become immortal because they exist *against* the world. Poems are salves. Contemporary lyric poetry is an antidote to the lived conditions that emerge from relationships between people and labour and institutions. This history of these relations is also the history of the production of the autonomous, atomised, ideal subject of the liberal order (a subject predicated on the exclusion of the feminised and racialised 'Other'). Or maybe poetry sits opposed to something even less tangible. Sometimes I think this 'something' is narrative itself. That is, the formal function of narrative as indexical to a historicised concept of society that can be traced alongside its development. While this function of narrative gives us rich material from which to contemplate the human condition at various points of history, the formal function of poetry offers us a way to interrogate the conditions of how meaning is produced. Contemporary lyric does this by foregrounding a subjectivity that slips between the individual and collective; it troubles the linearity that narrative implies. Poetry demands something of its readers that forms a bond of meaning-making between poems and those encountering them. Narrative neatens, while poetry atomises. The aesthetic possibilities of poetry might be wild or constrained to extreme proportions – it atomises our relationship to meaning itself by encouraging an experimentation that takes us to the edge of language's limits.

Each of us is individually forced to negotiate the terms of the capitalist system we have been pitted against. Some more than others. It gets hard sometimes. Through our class positions we are each limited by the constraints of our labour relations – wage, care – in ways that isolates us from community. It breeds abjection. My poetry is an antidote to my own abjection but only when I write it. I cannot say what it is when you read it. But the truth is, poetry is probably the only written form I would trust in a revolution.

—

When I became a poet I was already becoming a communist.

I've heard people referred to as a 'true poet' and fear that I am not that kind of poet. I don't really want to be a *true poet* anyway. I'm a communist poet.

Bernadette Mayer wrote *Midwinter Day* over the course of one day in 1978. It is a poem that embodies her practice: work, motherhood, domesticity, writing, Marxism. It is a formative poem for me.

It turns out the answer to the problem of poetry's secrecy is community. In a poetry community we talk about writing and share our work with each other. We collaborate on chapbooks, read poems out loud to each other occasionally. The secret is that it doesn't need to be secret.

—

I once nearly wrote a poem about the complexities of Desi women raised in cities such as Sydney. This is because I was living in Sydney and also because I had forgotten what my hometown Brisbane was (the place where my immigrant family lives). It had been years since I'd felt remotely 'Indian' (though I did try to write a poem about the gross response of Hindu nationalists to a Wendy Doniger book). I couldn't write fraudulently. That is, I couldn't write to my 'Indianness', which was diasporic, which felt disingenuously performative if I tried to invoke it in writing. Since my father died, though, I've been contemplating his homeland – not in Malaysia where he was born and raised, but Kerala, where the Indian Communist Party formed and where his father was orphaned and adopted. But to attempt to think about these things in poetry would still feel fraudulent – as though it were a performance for the white literary community. Anyway, it's not fraud that I'm interested in, but artifice.

Lately, I've been reading Veronica Forrest-Thomson on this subject. In *Poetic Artifice* she drills and drills and drills down into words. She's fierce about what poetry – 'the most garrulous study that exists' – is, and what it does that other literary forms cannot do. Forrest-Thomson observes language as belonging to the ordinary world as well as poetry, and that it is from ordinary language 'upon which Artifice must work to create its alternative imaginary orders'. Language can be decoupled from ordinariness to fulfil a poem's aesthetic destiny. She carved out a critical space for poems to be read not only for their thematic content but also their formal and aural content. She has been criticised by later poetry critics for misreading poems in ways that seemed to weaken her argument, but her attention to the relationship between poetry and language and what makes words 'natural' or how to fashion words for artifice have become fecund ground for me as I edit and rework my poems. Peter Riley has noted that Forrest-Thompson used 'the full forces [of ugliness and beauty] available in order to isolate the poem from the world as a privileged area of free play'. It is this sense of poetry as both a space for play as well as a space where language rules matter that guides my poem writing, which by necessity involves rewriting. There are some methods of artifice that I'm equipped to enact, and some that are beyond my comprehension. I notice a sense of work within the playfulness of writing poems.

The truth is, I have a sort of communist aversion to labour. I am sympathetic to William Morris's distinction in *Useful Work vs Useless Toil*:

> *Whatever pleasure there is in some work, there is certainly some pain in all work, the beast-like pain of stirring up our slumbering energies to action, the beast-like dread of change when things are pretty well with us; and the compensation for this animal pain is animal rest.*

Like most subjects under capitalism, I must exchange my labour power on the market. This is the source of my animal pain. (See also: white supremacy, rampant sexism.) Poetry is not *work*, but it must reckon with my beast-like pain and dread. It is my animal rest.

'The We of a Position' by Wendy Trevino begins like this:

I started to make a list of things that have happened, beginning with 'global financial crisis' & ending with me standing here in Oakland, reading something about labor, writing & fighting. Without even trying to include everything, I ran out of steam by the time I got to the third instance of 'looking for work' and the first word of students occupying UC buildings.

Trevino's beast-like pain and dread has a purpose: she channels it into 'writing & fighting'. Her poems are fighty; they think about cruelty but are not cruel themselves. If poems could be weapons against cruel politics, maybe Trevino can make them. Trevino's book is about cruel fictions:

A border, like race, is a cruel fiction
Maintained by constant policing, violence
Always threatening a new map...

Then again, as Roberto Bolaño once wrote, 'There is a time for reciting poems and a time for fists.'

—

I keep remembering poets I've been reading lately, like Jasmine Gibson and Trisha Low. My poetry used to be 'concerned with' excess but I think I had confused my inability to prune my poems effectively with some sort of blatant critique on contemporary consumer capitalism. I thought I could do Lara Glenum's 'gurlesque' and write poems about the grotesque, about women's bodies (my body), about warped beautiful things, about revolution and care labour. Forgive this simplistic description but the poems

I wrote back then contained these things. And yet when you read Jasmine Gibson's 'Hot-Hand Fallacy', it becomes apparent how a skilled poet plays with these elements of excess. Her poems are long and lush and full of big scenes, but there's a controlled manipulation of sounds and words too. Like when the narrator of the poem remembers getting a fat lip on a car door: 'I thought I'd lose a tooth and future suitors'. Thought and tooth phonetically pair, as well as 'lose', 'tooth' '*fu*ture', '*suit*ors'. These words feel like they should knock against each other, but they don't. The poem goes on to do other remarkable things, but this one line catches me sometimes, unexpectedly. And then there's her poem 'Kaddish', which opens with 'The world blew up in my mouth' and goes on with 'dark blood magic' and 'twisted cosmology' and 'manic limbo' and violence and bodies and violence against bodies (the raced body, the renter's body). The thing is, your own poetry doesn't exist alone. I keep remembering poets I've been reading as I make my own poems. These practices cannot be disentangled from each other. I write as a poet, as someone interested in realms of Marxist feminism, historical materialism, conditions of labour and gender that shape our lives. My reading and writing are explicitly collective, my poetics a slippage of 'I' and 'we', a poetics of citation and work, of subverting the oikos.

The poets I read over and over are ghosts in my poems. I write towards their collective body of works.

—

I get obsessed with things. When I became enamoured by cephalopods and molluscs they started appearing in my poems. This began with my reading *The Soul of an Octopus* by Sy Montgomery, which introduced me to the complexities of octopuses and turned my attention to how alien-like octopuses are. While we as a society often go to lengths to anthropomorphise the animals we encounter (remember the kangaroo who was thought to be grieving for its sickly mate, but who turned out to be attempting coitus?), Montgomery notices that the intelligence these cephalopods possess is unearthly and far from human (although she too falls into the trap of anthropomorphising these creatures by going in search of the creature's 'soul' and characterising the various octopuses she meets in ways that bring their personalities to life). Amia Srinivasan notes that '[t]he octopus threatens boundaries', which goes some way to explaining its amorphous appeal for me. I am no longer obsessed with these animals with the same intensity as back then, but I enjoy thinking about them often. (There are molluscs on the cover of my poetry book. *The Mollusk* is also the name of an album by Ween that I listened to a lot in my early twenties. Inked on my left forearm is a woman in a ball gown riding a giant snail.)

When I write poetry I'm not making a conscious sense of the world around me, but rather responding to it in ways that I'm not always able to comprehend – these responses can latch on to objects and animals. I wonder sometimes if the octopus held appeal for me because it offered me a way to conceptualise intelligence and curiosity in a way that seemed 'pure'. By zeroing in on the wonder of their existence, their home in the depths of the ocean might, albeit briefly, appear unmoored from the unbearable state of the world. This sense of the world as unbearable has given rise to another, more crucial obsession – anti-capitalism.

Poetry is my antidote for living under capitalism, one way to dabble in reading political economy and Marxist feminism. Even if poetry for me is emphatically *not work*, writing it sometimes takes on the qualities of work: guilt at not producing enough; or the frustration of missing out on awards (and the welcome cash spike it brings). It takes on the qualities of work when writers are exploited, for example, or when writers' access to publication and material benefits are determined by structures of class and white supremacy and patriarchy. And how poetry and so-called progressive corners of the arts are never immune to these structures.

In the past few years I've been researching Marxist feminism and poetics as part of a Masters of Fine Arts. Trying to knit together labour, care, poetry, gender, love, social reproduction; thinking about how these things inform each other. The refrain I keep returning to when I am thinking and writing is how capitalism conditions us; how it shapes our experience of survival vis-à-vis our various genders and classes and proximity to whiteness. My practice has transformed as needed, from exploratory and subconscious to purposeful and clarifying – it has moved in the liminal spaces of writing as a solitary practice (early-morning writing sessions, the clarity thoughts and words take on after prolonged periods alone) and poetry as a communal mode of being (our friendships, physical and digital circuits of publications, gathering in public for poetry readings, chapbook collaborations). And though finishing a four-year poetry research project might have potentially 'ruined' these subjects for me, I still find joy in re-reading Diane di Prima's *Revolutionary Letters* – a collection that has been republished multiple times over the decades that reinforces the enduring relevance of anti-capitalist poetry by showing us how such poetry's ability to respond to capitalism over time is as malleable and adaptable as capitalism itself.

Poetry and labour and social reproduction are inseparable. I write around and against doing laundry; draining lentils from a tin to add to rocket leaves, olive oil and salt to take to work; changing the bed sheets; feeding my cat. Others write around caring for children or family members or feeding their whole household.

One day I'd like to be the kind of poet who never gets asked about my day job. Ideally it will be because we have abolished wage labour.

Works Cited

Roberto Bolaño, *The Savage Detectives*, tr. Natasha Wimmer (New York: Farrar, Straus and Girroux, 2007).

Veronica Forrest-Thomson, *Poetic Artifice*, (Manchester: Manchester University Press, 1978; this edition published in Bristol: Shearsman Books, 2016, ed. Gareth Farmer).

Jasmine Gibson, *Don't Let Them See Me Like This* (Brooklyn: Nightboat Books, 2018).

Lara Glenum, *Maximum Gaga* (Notre Dame: Action Books, 2009).

Sy Montgomery, *The Soul of An Octopus* (New York: Atria Books, 2015).

William Morris, *Useful Work vs. Useless Toil* (Sydney: The Judd Publishing Co., 1919).

Fred Moten, 'barbara lee [the poetics of political form]' in *B Jenkins* (Durham: University Press, 2010).

Peter Riley, 'Poetry Notes', *Fortnightly Review*, 4 May 2014.

Amia Srinivasan, 'The Sucker, The Sucker!', *London Review of Books*, vol. 3, no. 17, 7 September 2017.

Wendy Trevino, *Cruel Fiction* (Oakland: Commune Editions, Oakland, 2018).

Lifting
Maddee Clark

At Macquarie University's Indigenous Futurisms conference, Gomeroi writer Alison Whittaker speaks about publishing her first book of poetry. She tells us about being in unstable housing, and desperately needing money at the time she made the book deal. She says she was completely unprepared for the experience of writing about traumatic and personal events in her life, and then being asked about those experiences again and again for a year at panels and writer's festivals.

The conference takes place on a sweaty day at the Redfern Community Centre. It's an environment where no one is cagey about talking about the money they make as a writer. Prior to Alison taking the stage, Noongar writer Claire Coleman notes her disappointment with trauma writing, saying she believes Aboriginal people should stop writing about trauma for a public audience altogether. The audience chews on this with a bit of resistance. We're all prepared to acknowledge that even if you're not a poet, self-exposure makes money in the age of the confessional personal essay. Exposure of your own bullshit, your trauma, your secrets, is a marketable practice. As a group, however, we're not completely settled on whether trauma writing is useful – for the reader or the writer.

When I don't want to write, I watch *The Wendy Williams Show*. Wendy opens her show every day with a celebrity gossip segment called 'Hot Topics', where she gives hot takes on different celebrity scandals: relationship breakdowns, pregnancies, addictions, court cases, and anything else that has been dragged out into the public eye.

She takes the same attitude towards her own life. Wendy filed for divorce from her husband in April 2019, but for some time before this, when rumours were going around that he was being unfaithful, she defended him publicly on 'Hot Topics'. Every time the rumours came up, she would address them openly to her live audience, declaring that, 'It's me that's the hot topic!' She talks about knowing that even though her marriage has ended in betrayal, she has confirmed an eleventh season of her show while her ex is now going to be changing nappies. 'My mother taught me how to make lemonade out of lemons,' she says. She explains her decision to share her story with the audience, with her logic amounting to something like: 'If I expose everyone else, I have to expose myself too':

You wear a different mask when you're out here. Everybody, including you, whether you're a secretary or a schoolteacher or whatever, everybody has things in their life that they are embarrassed to share with the world, that they're frightened to share with the world, that they're not ready to share with the world...the motto of this show will always be; their business is...

to which the audience responds: 'Our business!' And everyone applauds.

Wendy's been on television doing a daily show for over a decade. I wonder whether the moments of disclosure – her struggles with addiction, the betrayal of her partner and co-parent, and her sometimes destructive relationship with fame – are helpful for her, or if they're just part of the show. Either way, she's adept at utilising these moments of suffering to generate ratings, to add fuel to her own flame. She's able to create the impression of being completely open, while presumably holding a little of something back. It's something I feel incapable of.

Being a writer with no money means that it becomes tempting to use your emotional vulnerability and self-exposure to offset your financial vulnerability. I'm uncomfortable being vulnerable. I'm uncomfortable with other people's vulnerability too. I don't like to admit that I need the money I get from writing. Writing is something I do to heal myself, and having been broke and homeless before, much of that healing coalesces around the pay cheque, when I get it. Once I started getting paid for writing, my mental health improved quickly. I try to make money out of criticism, arts writing, book reviews, copy text for *whatever*; anything that doesn't involve talking about myself, until talking about (or criticising) other people becomes a habit that I feel I can't evolve out of.

I struggle with addiction, like Wendy does. When I get sober, I start going to the gym, and with all my new spare time and predisposition for extremity and addictive behaviours, I begin competing in powerlifting. Powerlifting is a sport which, much like bodybuilding, as Marcia Ian has pointed out, is 'dedicated to wiping out "femininity," insofar as femininity has for centuries connoted softness, passivity, non-aggressivity, and physical weakness'.

Strength sports, by definition, reject vulnerability, declaring a commitment to the development of mental and physical toughness. Women's participation in powerlifting, historically an aggressively male sport, has increased by four times in the last decade alone, and continues to rise exponentially, forcing a rearticulation of the gender politics of the sport. Queer women participate in droves.

Trans, intersex, and otherwise gender non-conforming women

have been the subject of an increasingly heated discussion in the sporting world lately. Being a trans man, and nowhere near strong enough to win any medals, I escape most of this scrutiny, aside from a continuing negotiation with the anti-doping authorities over my use of testosterone for gender transition rather than for cheating (testosterone, of course, plays its own supplementary role in bodybuilding's cultural rejection of femininity and physical softness).

The gym becomes the place I want to write about. I go with my girlfriend to an old-school powerlifting and strongman gym in Aotearoa. The gym owner is huge and friendly. He tells us that this gym is mainly a working-class gym, and is usually completely empty during the day, only busy early in the morning or after work hours. However, on this particular day, a men's rugby team is training in here. The women's bathrooms are permanently out of order, so one stall in the very back corner of the men's bathroom is reserved for women. When I go in to use it, one of the players is in there peeing with the door open. The walls of the gym are plastered thick with laminated A4 typed sheets of paper explaining the 'Rules', both gym etiquette and those pertaining to correct eating, training, and the requisite attitude adjustments needed to get strong: 'Remember, somewhere in the world, a little girl is warming up with your max!'

Kathy Acker wrote that bodybuilding, for her, was a rejection of ordinary language. There was an 'antagonism' between language and the gym that prevented her from writing about it easily: 'after every workout, I forgot to write. Repeatedly. I...some part of me...the part of the "I" who bodybuilds...was rejecting language.' For Acker, working out is an escape from words into mindless repetition, into the logics of the body. The gym is seen as antithetical to writing and intellect. The body doesn't write, or if it does, it does so in another language. I don't relate. I do most of my good writing at the gym, feeding off the extremities and horniness that gym contains. I wonder how much of my co-workers and friends learned fearfulness and disbelief at my gym habits is a class-based response. The divide between the intellectual class and the working class, after all, has always been a body/mind split; the body does, the brain thinks. When I decided to go to university, my dad sat me down to tell me that he wasn't book smart. That it was okay if I wasn't too, that there's no shame in a normal job, as long as you're working. As long as you have something to do. There's nothing worse than having nothing to do.

I bring a friend to the gym and they joke that they must be the only jock at the gym who carries a book with them in their gym bag. Over twenty years after Acker wrote about bodybuilding, the archetypal gym bro has expanded his gaze. Critical thinking is now valued. The ideal lifter is now an energy efficient technician. The line between the jock and the nerd is getting thinner. A type of snobbery takes hold, especially among powerlifters who want their practice to be seen as more discerning and science-based than the 'gen pop'. Kathy Acker, after all, asserted her own bodybuilding processes of repetition, destruction and growth to be similar to the formula for an art practice.

I compete in the men's division of my drug-tested federation for the first time on 24 November last year. A week later, I see another trans man post about competing in the same federation as me. It is reposted by another trans advocate from the United States, a trans woman who is an athlete in the USAPL, a federation which has gone against the ruling of the International Olympic Committee by placing a blanket ban on trans athletes. Me and the local trans guy chat a little and follow each other online. A few weeks later, he reposts a meme to his page. It is plain black text on white, and it reads: 'Sending love to everyone who's trying their best to heal from things that they don't fucking discuss!!' The author adds a note: 'including me!'

Paper Princess
McKenzie Wark

People often ask me why it is that I write so much. I never know what to say. I'm back home in Australia, on a flying visit from New York. The colour of the leaves, the birdsong, everything is tugging at my senses, bringing me back to a past that's becoming nebulous, fantastic as the years in New York pile on.

My sister takes me to the storage unit that holds some lost chunk of my Australian life. There's the metal shelves I spent two days assembling. There's the double rows of books, slightly random, abandoned and sad. I don't really care what happens to them anymore.

I'm digging through it all for the few more personal things I might still care about. Here's the old metal tin. In it, letters from former lovers. I leaf through them, glance at the handwriting. I know they all complain about the same thing. That the writer cannot reach me, that I remain hidden from them. Well, I was hidden from myself, hun. It gives me no satisfaction to know this now.

Among the letters, a postcard. A picture of an institutional building. Somehow, I know it's a hospital. I turn the card over. It is my mother's handwriting. She is writing to me from this hospital. The last place she was ever to be.

I'm smash cut into a memory of visiting her in it. We took the long ride from Newcastle down the old Pacific Highway to Sydney. I am six years old. The ride bores me. We pass the exit sign for Crow's Nest. Funny name for a place, I say. I'm asked to be quiet. My father is trying not to get lost.

I've brought something to show my mother in the hospital. A paper cone, coloured in with my coloured pencils. There's a flat paper head attached. She is a princess. Maybe I made her at Sunday school. We are not a religious family. I was being sent across the road to the Baptist Sunday school to get me out of the house – give my father and older siblings a break from me. I think about this sometimes. What it must have been like. They all knew she was dying.

I'm holding my paper princess. I see that my colouring is not quite as good as I'd like. I missed a bit. But I don't have my pencils. I show her to my mother. The feeling that remains, from this event, long ago, is one of disappointment. That her reaction wasn't anything. I can now put myself in her place a little, but I don't let myself dwell on what she could have felt, to see her youngest child, a little grumpy from the car ride, but chattering away, as if nothing was happening, while knowing that this child will soon be motherless in the world. I am older now than she was then. I have kids of my own. If I think about this too much, her pain becomes mine.

There is none of this in the postcard she wrote me from this hospital. Its tone is light and chatty. Written to a child, in the loopy hand that reminds me of my sister's. I asked my sister to tell me a bit about our mother. I remember very little. This memory from the hospital is one of exactly nine memories I have of her. My sister told me that Joyce Wark was brave and proud and reserved, that she didn't let her feeling show, that she went out of this life keeping her suffering to herself.

It's strange, this postcard – delivered back, from me to me, via storage unit. I have no memory of it. How do you forget the one thing your dead mother ever wrote to you? That it even exists? I brought it back to New York with me. I look at it sometimes. What else falls out of memory? Sometimes I doubt any of us have any idea who we are at all.

I am sitting at *Public Records*, a café and bar in Brooklyn, with my friend Jackie. She has her notebook out. I am writing this on my laptop. My phone's timer is on. We're free writing together, across from each other. I don't want her to see me cry.

The one thing I know best about my mother is her taste in literature. Her books filled the house, long after she was gone. My father gave a brace of her hardbacks away once, and I was furious with him, although I did not know why. I think now that the books were my link to her. I read them to find her.

She had a taste for literary modernism. I contracted that taste from the yellowing pages of her books. She even had Joyce's *Ulysses*, which was banned in Australia for a very long time. I especially loved the bright orange jackets, slightly faded, of old Penguin paperbacks. She was a reader. That's really about all I know about her.

Another of my handful of memories of her: a time she took me to Cardiff public library. We are in the children's section. It was after play school, where she took me one morning a week. I liked it there, but there were two little girls I wanted to play with, and I never could, until one day they invited me to tea under the slippery dip. But it started to rain and we were all called inside and I was sad because I did not get to join their tea party game.

After play school, the library. Maybe she took me to cheer me up that day. I remember my mother as a warm presence, a benign ambience, but I don't have an image of her. All I remember of the library is the bright colours of the books, in rows, in racks: reds, yellows, blues. Some exotic looking books in purple and orange. I had to choose just one book, but I wanted them all.

Writing is what my mother gave me. She must have given me other things. I was loved. I feel that this has to be true. I have no way of knowing other than the evidence of my body, my life – that I can love and let myself be loved, even when I've not loved much of myself. Writing is the thing that she gave me that I can remember, at least a little. Writing is what left traces. In my love of reading, in the library she left, and in the postcard, that I kept, and forgot.

Becoming a writer filled the solitude left by her leaving. I know that she did not abandon me. She had cancer. Feelings don't always answer to reason. Sometimes they just make a void around themselves and remain, undetected. When I started transition and went on hormones, the past all came back to me, came out of its nothingness. All the loss, all the longing, all the pain, and with it this time, at least, an understanding of this compulsion to write, this refuge in writing. When I am writing, I am always writing to my mother.

Another memory: my mother and I are visiting her parents in Ashfield, a suburb of Sydney. My father isn't there – he never comes. It's just the two of us and my maternal grandparents who I barely remember and who seemed remote and scary. We're on a big bed together and my mother just read me that Winnie the Pooh story where he attaches himself to a balloon and flies into the air to steal honey from the bees. The bees don't fall for it, and Piglet has to get Christopher Robin to come and shoot Pooh down.

She read me that story. I remember this because I read the

same story to my own daughter and the pictures brought it back to me. I didn't like the story. I didn't like the ending, so I made my mother tell it a different way. And the balloon had to be orange – my favorite colour. I could not read yet, and my minor motor skills were so poor I could not colour within the lines – but in that moment, I became a writer.

For fifty years I've been answering her postcard. Telling her about the books I read and how they could go differently. And, finally, I had to write to her about how I could go differently. I had to not just come out as a transsexual, in the world, but in writing. Only now I've lost her twice, lost into a deeper solitude. She wasn't there for the childhood where everyone thought I was a boy and even I believed it too. And now she is not there for the childhood that I did not have, as a girl. The letters that she is not there to receive are from someone else who she is not there to not recall. But I keep sending them, as I always have. As I need to do.

For thirty years I've written into the void using the name McKenzie Wark. I never really knew why. McKenzie is my middle name. It was my maternal grandmother's maiden name. I feel certain now that of my two given names, it's the one my mother chose. Maybe I use it as a signal, or sigil, flung across blank forgetting so she would know it is me and that I need her. Need her at least to have been.

The timer went off. I stopped typing on my laptop. Jackie put down her pen. Dub music filled the space – the DJ had started while we were writing. Gorgeous deep cuts, beyond the reach of Shazam. Lost in the stringing of sentences, I hadn't noticed although it probably entered the rhythm of typing. We left *Public Records* and set off on foot, across Brooklyn, to the Brooklyn Bridge, to Manhattan. Jackie wanted to show me her favourite bookstore – *Two Bridges* – tucked away on the second story of a Chinatown mall. And I loved it. Except that it didn't carry any of my books.

I Want to Live in A Classless Society
Ellena Savage

My skin is white, or rather it is a soft, warm pink, which is the colour of the skin of the most dangerous and successful pillagers in recent times. I descend from them. I am them. Nothing is random. I am capable of killing another person but I would prefer not to. I would prefer not to survive an apocalypse.

My parents and siblings are all alive. None have ever been to prison. None have ever abused me, or each other, to my knowledge, unless you count light-to-moderate corporal punishment, which I don't, though I think it should be banned. Both my parents have read *Jane Eyre*. I cried a lot in girlhood, mostly over infractions that were described to me as 'spilt milk'. There have always been books in my house. I have hunted for feral cats, unsuccessfully. I have never slaughtered an animal. I have always felt the presence of a force with designs on my exiguous freedom. I enjoy the liberties of adulthood considerably.

I don't know where, exactly, my family originates from. Both my grandmothers were liars. Neither of my grandmothers were, historically speaking, lucky. My mother is becoming interested in genealogy. She discovered a somewhat recent ancestoress who birthed seven children, then died at thirty-four. Historically speaking, this woman was not a lucky woman. Most people who have ever lived and died were not, historically speaking, lucky people. I, on the other hand, am the luckiest woman to have ever been born. I am thirty-one years old.

Luck makes no sense. Interventionist gods do not exist. Barbara Baynton – author, liar, gold-digger, survivor – delivered her own baby, alone, in a shed in the bush with no running water. There are few historico-spatial windows in which people like me have not had to be pregnant and nursing for the duration of their reproductive lives, and I live in the middle of one. Barbara Baynton also opposed (white) women's suffrage. Survivors of historical cruelty can be politically incorrect too. There is no precedent for someone like me to have access to a public in which to exhibit her uniqueness. Yet here I am, unique.

All my grandparents are dead. I am estranged from most members of my extended family. Many of my relatives lived, or live, with obsessions and addictions, and I am aware of what this might tell me about my own genetic predilections.

I have a lot to live for. I would like to write one decent book. I would like to earn a living from teaching. I enjoy getting drunk with my friends. I am a 'people person'. My monthly prescription costs six dollars fifty. I am loved.

The worst feature of human society is servitude. I would like there to be a social revolution but I would prefer not to live through it. I don't cry often but when I do it is with gusto. The last time I cried, I cried for days. I lay on the wooden floor and slapped my palm against it in a melodramatic fashion. The action was involuntary, yet it felt delicious and indulgent. I have been financially independent since I was eighteen. I am not particularly responsible, but I'm not profligate, either. I forgo exercise when on a deadline.

My most useful personal quality is that I am practical. I don't mind being disliked. I don't mind cleaning up vomit. I can turn three dollars into a nutritious meal.

I have no 'full' cousins. My closest cousin is a fundamentalist

Muslim revert. She unfriended me on Facebook after our grandmother's funeral at Auburn Mosque, which I did not attend, because before dying, our grandmother disowned my father in a way I found heartless and unjustified. I care about the author behind the work. I care about the signifieds. The question of who a speech act is addressing tells me all I need to know. I don't know what it feels like to love God, but I am attracted to the idea. I know how to load and shoot a double barrel shotgun.

To critique an act of kindness for the value it bestows the bestower is to misunderstand the human need to be helpful. To never engage in sexualised labour is, for a woman, to fail at working under patriarchy. Sex workers know this. Trade unionists should know this. Writing is easier, more pleasurable, than most paid work is. Teaching is as hard as waitressing, but the conditions are much better. People who use Melbourne Central train station should honour escalator conventions more thoroughly. Extending one's middle finger is often the correct answer to the question. When a stranger coughs in public, one should move six feet away to avoid the bacterial sillage.

My least useful quality is I don't like being made fun of. Some people find this a reason to make fun of me, which I can see the humour in but don't enjoy.

I have eaten frog legs and fried grasshoppers. Both taste green in different ways. I am a bad actress. I could never be a spy, which is what spies must say to their lovers. I don't like writing fiction because I fail to understand the difference between fantasy and construction. I harshly judge dishonesty, most of all self-deception. Yet I like to big-note myself. I like to feel that my choices are difficult. I am gifted at certain forms of human closeness. My husband calls me 'the good wife' after a self-sacrificing television wife who unshackles herself to become independently rich and morally corrupt. My relationship to animals is one of distant yet mighty respect. I am protective of people younger than me. The living writers I most admire are Jamaica Kincaid and Maria Tumarkin. I hold two powerful passports.

Last financial year I earned $34,769 AUD. In raw terms, this puts me in the world's wealthiest 2.6%. In less raw terms, not so much. I know that time to write costs money, but this claim depends on a condition of entitlement to a future pool of unreal money that I don't possess. I want to live in a society that is not obsessed with work. I know I am a dispensable person, economically speaking. Although I know that nostalgia is dangerous, I allow it to influence my decisions. One of my former best friends no longer speaks to me. Doubtless there are others who no longer speak to me, but I don't speak to them either.

I was raised to believe that a 'healthy' ego is one that lays supine before the authoritarian Madam superego. I am embarrassed for those who make a habit of bragging. I am often embarrassed for myself. I object to the term 'imposter syndrome', because it assumes that the native and desirable state for human activity is mastery and arrogance. I don't believe in absolution, that the forgiven are truly forgiven. I do believe in getting on with it; I believe in living with ghosts. I worry about my parents' physical and financial future but I don't do anything to help. They hide twenty dollar notes in my purse when I go to the bar to buy a round of drinks for them. Part of me believes that it is up to the highest-earning sibling to help the parents, and I am not that. Soon, all of my parents' children will live in nations far from them, a fact I am one-third responsible for.

I am concerned I have reached the summit of my intellectual potential, and the view from it is jankier than I'd hoped. I find myself circling the same questions again, each time thinking myself wiser, each time unable to answer them with any more conviction. I am more productive when someone I love has been cruel to me. People who regularly eat luxury café foods on weekends should not say that they are 'poor'. Australians are a uniquely stingy people.

My student debt sits at $30,598. On two occasions, working data entry for a groovy corporate publisher, I was paid enough to have to make payments against it. Each day, after lunch, I cried silently at my desk. After two pay cheques, I was fired. Lately I have been feeling financially comfortable. I own four dresses by a designer I like. Recycling will not fix anything. Writing will not fix anything. I will not receive an inheritance aside from a few good jazz records. My view that inheritance should be abolished and replaced with a classless social structure could therefore be construed as convenient. It is unlikely that I will have children. It is necessary to let go of the idea of the future as an untrammelled past.

At all times, I have at least one bruise, burn, or graze on my body. I have been in love more times than is socially acceptable at this particular historical matrix. I have never been in love with a person who belonged to someone else. I know that possessive language in the love arena is a language of coercion, of patriarchy, of control. I also know that being possessed is a fact of being seen, and known, by someone else. Like Ado Annie, I give my consent freely, when I can, to almost anything.

I frequently fall over while walking on cobblestone laneways. I find some aspects of urban conservation suspect. I did a PhD to pay for time to write and then I spent too much time writing a not-great PhD thesis. Supermarket dips offend me. I am more concerned by how bureaucracies naturalise subject-object relations between humans than I am by the abstract destruction of the environment. I became more sexually conservative after reading Michel Foucault's *The History of Sexuality*. I want to live in a society that is classless, but one that can tolerate beauty. I want to live in a classless society.

Park Office

Tom Lee

The car helped enable the suburb to become a widespread landscape format, thereby blurring the previously discrete conceptions of the town and the country. Portable computing technology is having comparable, if yet-to-crystallise effects on the places people live, play and work. Particularly those of us engaged in the so-called knowledge economy. We already have the neologism '*coffice*', a designation that names the practice of people adapting cafés for the purpose of work. But this is just one example of a place – or really two places – being remade through the affordances of mobile computing. The home/office binary is a relatively crude rendering in comparison.

While the scale and quality of such technologically oriented changes to human practices are often riven with misapprehension, I cannot help but consider – from my privileged vantage in a picnic hut overlooking Bronte beach – that the modern office is an artefact from a time when work needed to be conducted in a different manner and atmosphere, and that now, unlocked from the brightly lit, uncomfortable, stifling, energy-intensive, disease spreading, anxiety-inducing structures in which work commonly took place over the last century, we ought to start thinking very differently about what a place of work might be. It is easy to see the backwardness of brutal, smoke-filled nineteenth- and early twentieth-century factories. Perhaps in the latter parts of the twenty-first century, the modern office and its associated scenography will appear similarly dated?

I belong to a fortunate demographic who is able to enjoy

both security and flexibility in my occupation. As an academic, my work is made up of a combination of teaching, research and administrative duties. A fair portion of my day involves responding to internal emails, reading and writing for research, assessing student applications, marking and curriculum development, and various online acrobatics associated with different digital administrative systems. Much of this can be executed through the little, illuminated portal of my computer screen. There is no need for such antisocial behaviour to take place in the often similarly antisocial confines of an office.

So instead of the office, I choose parks, at least for some portion of the day. I'm a regular inhabitant of Bronte Park, in the early morning, where I enjoy the shelter and the thick cement tables in the picnic huts and the incomparable brain refreshment of a dip in the ocean. Later in the day, I take up residence in Prince Alfred Park, which is close enough to my place of work for my fleshy form to manifest in the corridors in a matter of minutes. These adapted office-parks suggest vast spectrum of working spaces where leisure and labour mix in new ways. While the steady diffusion of work into previously foreign realms isn't always a laudatory phenomenon, in this little speculative adventure, I'm going to focus on some of the more positive possibilities in part afforded by our digital possibles.

—

I scan the ground in Prince Alfred Park, making calculations based on gradient, shade and, to a lesser extent, the quality of the grass. The landscape I observe is completely different to the range of support structures for the human body that are commonly found in offices. In my work office, the chair is a discrete object, clearly identifiable from the context in which it is placed. It goes together with the desk, the height of which is synchronised with the chair. My office has been made explicit. The air is conditioned. The building affords shade from overhead sunlight. Everything has been prepared.

In the park, however, I must work to distinguish my chair from its surrounds. Here my office is implicit. There is a range of sloped, shaded areas where I can comfortably lie down on my back, prop my laptop up on my knees and work. The slope and the shade are both important: no shade and the screen is hard to see and the sun hurts my eyes; no slope and the flat ground requires that I have to prop my neck up at a sharp angle to see the screen and work the keyboard. Ideally, the area of grass I find is lush and thick enough to protect me from smudges of dirt, though not so long that it encourages the presence of insects who bite the soft, sensitive skin that is characteristic of my species.

In this particular park office, there is no table and chair, just a comparatively vast, undulating surface into which I temporarily fit my body and its computing appendage. I imagine a similar park dotted with deliberate impressions in the shape of the human form, little ergonomic ditches, each with its own tree which throws a bobble of shade over the moulded ground. I imagine different configurations of these ditches, some are isolated, some are connected in small, radial forms. Bodies slot into these ditches, they fold themselves down into the earth in a posture that is appropriate for an interfacial relationship with a screen.

The longer I stay lying on the grass to work, the further my possessions seem to spread out around me. It's as though the force of gravity is gradually realising its impact and causing my things to disperse. I bring my knees up towards my chest and chock my laptop in between my torso and my thighs. My arms are folded in close to my body and my hands hang over the keyboard, a little like the front paws of a kangaroo. I imagine a *plein air* painter, perhaps Marie Mansfield, working on another painting for her captivating series depicting the bodies of sprawled office workers in parks in the city. The details of my posture are crucial: my semi-formal office clothes; the internal tension of my posture, with the suggestion of lassitude evoked by a splayed limb; the contrasting sense of a body at once exposed in open space and yet immersed, not in the physical space as such, but in the microworld formed between mind and screen.

I can't bring myself to lie down while inside at work. An invisible but active barrier exists that requires I stand or sit. The chairs and tables and the observed norms of my colleagues induce a reasonably strong sense that lying down in the workplace would demand an explanation that I'm yet to perfect.

While standing and writing is increasingly common, and walking meetings are a growing trend, lying down to write or to talk in the office remains transgressive behaviour. A horizontal posture still signals leisure, nonchalance, a lack of willingness to perform.

Despite being an unusual spot to work, I am happy standing with my laptop at a cement ledge in an old, disused industrial goods line adjacent to the university campus. Sometimes I stand and spread out my things on one of the cement ping pong tables in a small outdoor area near the so-called alumni green. The large, flat, waist-high surface is a relatively unique outdoor affordance in the context of the university campus. There are a few trees nearby under which I occasionally lie under with my laptop, head propped up with a surprisingly comfortable, makeshift pillow composed from my backpack and a cup wedged underneath the back of my skull. On the other side of the alumni green there is a small, grassy slope with a rare bit of shade that is often occupied by groups of students. It seems two metres' distance between groups roughly sets the limits of etiquette with regard to personal space. I observe from the ping pong tables and make a move when a portion of grass becomes free.

Lying down and working remains very much an outdoor activity, more or less restricted exclusively to parks and green space. A supine body and a patch of grass seem to go together. In other public spaces, reclining is often treated as an improper sedentary practice. Recently I adopted my horizontal writing posture on a park bench to enjoy the ambivalent ambience of Henry Deane Plaza, just near Railway Square in Sydney. Before long, a tap on the shoulder burst the bubble that had formed between me and the screen. A security guard in dark clothes temporarily shaded my face from the sun. Apparently, sitting or standing was mandatory. My horizontal form was taking up too much room on the bench. I observed the three other empty benches and the largely deserted plaza in disbelief and moved on, hoping the lawn on alumni green might be free.

In the heat of the increasingly long summer, the park is often too hot. I'm tempted, occasionally, by the giant, cool edifice of Central Station not far from my office. I enjoy working in places of transit, the regular flows of people and the anonymity seem to induce the levity that comes with the romance of travel. But once I move inside the zone of the building, I no longer feel comfortable lying down on the ground. The atmosphere does not invite it. Even sitting in the space is a challenge. There are no public tables, and the few benches are hard and typically occupied. While one of the new cafés offers an appealing ambience in which to work, I typically have my own food and thermos in my backpack with which I am reluctant to part. I once asked in the café how much I would have to pay simply to use one of the tables. I told the staff that I'd be happy to pay the price of a coffee and a muffin to sit there and eat my own food. Unsurprisingly, they refused on the grounds of health and safety. Though a woman working there subsequently suggested that if I used one of the tables around the back, out of view, it would be okay. These tables, however, were in a dull little nook with no sense of the station atmosphere and its invitingly open, energised space. I sat out the front of the station on a thin strip of sloping grass under the shade of a tree instead.

I overhear another occupant of a Bronte picnic hut talk about how he'd started doing billable work from down at the beach. He is one of a group of three or four men who I see in the huts every morning. Their push bikes, clothes and water sports apparatus make the segment of the hut they occupy appear like the veranda of a well-lived-in home. Sometimes I get distracted listening to the conversation of these improvised colleagues. I hear of trips to Queenstown in New Zealand, of oyster preferences and of theories about how light projection works. One man has two dogs, a little chihuahua that he cradles in this arm and a larger, golden dog, who he is often telling off for bothering other people in the huts in search of food. I have built a sort of distant camaraderie with these men. Together we consistently exclaim that the water is beautiful, even on the most threatening and choppy days. Occasionally I see different people at work in the huts: a woman with a laptop who smiles at me after my swim, a man with a straw hat and newspaper spread over the table, an older couple with an elaborate kit for making health drinks.

The pigeons have cottoned on to my routine and they emerge not long after I arrive to peck the scraps of pastry from the ground beneath the table. Initially the presence of their feathered bodies networking in between my feet made me uncomfortable and I would kick and shoo them away. With time, however, we have become better acquainted with each other and now on the mornings they don't come I am sad and wonder where they are. The ibis too, patrol the ground, half-heartedly pecking the earth while training an eye on the crumpled paper bags that litter the table. Sometimes a magpie will come, always a little more timid than the other birds. It will point its beak upwards, skewering my gaze, and swivel its head slowly from side-to-side so I can see its orange-brown eyes, then erupt into piercingly beautiful song. I miss my animal friends in the corridors at work and it strikes me – in the speculative space this page allows me to conjure – how strange it is that we have banished other creatures from the places us city folk choose to labour.

The city office has to a significant degree been shaped by the towering, vertically-oriented buildings in the CBD, which allow many people to cluster in the one area. But as that need to some extent diminishes, different places of work suggest themselves as emergent forms in the landscape. I imagine the great, empty stadiums around the city filling with fellow travellers during the day, who come in search of shaded seating, basic amenities, recreational green space and a sense of occasion to enjoy while attending to emails.

Clusters of yet to be realised offices and places of revivification might compose our daily trajectories around the city. The work office and the home remain orienting forces, but increasing numbers of outdoor offices emerge in the zones of land in between and around these key destinations.

Occasionally I take the train from Central to Kings Cross and walk to Reg Bartley Oval at Rushcutters Bay, where the modest, shaded grandstand overlooking the sporting field and the harbour is a perfect vision of the city. There is an outdoor fitness gym nearby, and, of course, the oval, should I wish to exercise on a break. Not far away is Trumper Park, which features the same combination of accessibility from the station, a grandstand with seating and shade, toilets, recreational space, and a picturesque backdrop – this time bushland.

Frustratingly, Apple have already tarnished my vision and labeled their massive new headquarters in California, Apple Park. Rather than the rectilinear, high-rise icon of the twentieth century, the radial form of the stadium and the spaceship are the more conspicuous precedents for the structure. As the name suggests, however, more than anything else, it is an office that has the aspirations of park, where outdoor recreation and leisure in green space are valued as much as labouring away indoors.

Whether such aspirations are realised in the everyday practices and working conditions of its occupants is another matter, and indeed, one can imagine a tortuous situation where flogged workers remain in a state of endless yearning, the green interior garden a little dream of recreation, like the hastily purchased, rarely used, sporting apparatuses that clutter the garages of the perpetually busy. The office workers in Apple Park might be simultaneously tempted by and deprived of luxuriant green and fresh air while working non-stop throughout the day.

The future park-office I have in mind is a related yet contrasting vision to that of Apple Park. It involves vernacular adaptations of existing landscape features and minor, though precise elements of urban infrastructure, such as power points, comfortable and durable outdoor furniture, rudimentary sheltered areas, and, most importantly, lots of trees. Rather than remaining beholden to the residual temptations of gathering in an indoor office, co-workers might strike out together on little expeditions into such park offices and gradually find themselves acting in subtly different ways and feeling differently about their work. The look and feel of our parks will also change in the process. Like the crowds of fitness enthusiasts and personal training collectives, these computer augmented, mobile knowledge workers will be an increasingly common sights in our parks. A new conversational tone might emerge from the sprawled bodies, who are inhibited and enabled in certain ways by their vegetative posture and the indirect communicative relations it affords.

The modernist visions of co-isolated living in the twentieth century were in part inspired by the architecture of medieval monasteries. One of the greatest contributors to this collective imagining was Le Corbusier, who saw a perfect architectural image expressed in the Charterhouse of Ema at Galluzzo, a Cistercian monastery, where each inhabitant had his own, self-contained cell. Impractical romanticisations of the past have their limitations in a plainly different contemporary context. However, if European architects can turn to medieval monks for inspiration, then perhaps we in Australia ought look to the anthropological history of our landscape for ideal visions for living, remembering it was enjoyed as a beautifully and functionally designed space for outdoor living for tens of thousands of years by Indigenous Australians. Sadly, its stories may be less readily accessible, but as architects and landscape architects who are sensitive to climate, culture and landscape continue to demonstrate, the longer story of our landscape still persists, waiting for us to find our place within it, should we listen and look in a manner that deserves an invitation. It might seem as though we've already come a long way in this regard, with some clever developments in the way landscapes and interiors are integrated in functional, aesthetically pleasing spaces. However, as I watch an old, sun-leathered man carefully fix his towel to a steel fence by the beach with clothes pegs he brings each day specifically for this purpose – I think, perhaps we are only at the tip of an iceberg when it comes to changing the mix of the inside and the outside in the places we live, work and play.

A Glovebox of One's Own

Luke Carman

Henry Savery wrote the first novel published in Australia and he ended his story by slitting his throat 'from ear to ear' in a Port Arthur prison, convicted of returning to forgery to make ends meet. Another famous Henry once advised all budding Australian authors to flee for London or 'study elementary anatomy, especially as applies to the cranium, and then shoot themselves carefully with the aid of a looking-glass'. When I worked at the University teaching creative writing, my friend and fellow scribbler Martin Edmond, who had the excuse that he was born in New Zealand, used to come in and lecture the wide-eyed innocent undergrads that 'writers are the true proletariat', which I took to be a romantic way of trying to scare the smart ones straight, but those sweet babes hardly ever got the message.

One trick you must master, being a writer, is begging richer folk for their money. Institutions like to keep you around too, when you're good at beggary, so when the school of arts at a local university needed some cash one year, they gathered some of us writer-beggars for a soiree at a stupendously rich person's house, with tall shutter-flanked windows above a simple portico of grey stone set in brick veneer, and three topiary swans behind security guards using walkie-talkies to direct traffic onto a sweeping lawn with wild flowers round its circuitous perimeter. There were house staff wearing yellow fascinators out front by a trestle table, waving welcome to the many guests in frocks and coats, and we were stuck with name tags as we wandered by. Teams of waiters in grey suits and gloves made the consumption of free food and booze all the easier by bringing platters of rice paper rolls, crostini with marinated mushroom, and glasses of red and white wine. The gentleman who owned the place thanked us all for coming, said hello to the mayor, who held up a glass of champagne in salute, and the crowd of fine folk, writers, professors, and politicians were all invited to make themselves at home and inspect the private war museum out back, complete with a decommissioned tank. While we wandered and supped and smiled at each other, the evening's shadows sharpened under the orange lanterns on the stony walls and the flickering glow of tiki torches staked beyond the stony courtyard. Desserts were served with slips of bright bubbly and when we had finished our talks and readings, with some blushing about money, the hostess took to the balcony above the back portico to announce a violin was about to start playing from an open window in the eastern wing, in a room lit by a single red lamp, and the university gifted their host a signed hardcover copy of Alexis Wright's *Carpentaria*, and taking the book in hand the host said 'I've already got one of these, you gave me one last time', while everyone applauded.

The first woman I spoke to after all the official business wore an azure gown with bone-white swirls curling down her sides and long silver earrings hanging to her shoulders. She introduced herself, said she enjoyed the readings, and handed me a book to sign, and to my great surprise it was one I'd written. While I was signing, I tried some small talk, asking this smiling woman with wine-dark hair, 'What is it that you do?' She didn't want to say, fearing that, should her livelihood be uncovered, all the artist-types and academics would denounce her as a monster. This seemed interesting, so I tried a little harder and it turned out she was directly involved with the WestConnex project that was, and still is for all I know, under construction all over Sydney.

'I know,' she said grimacing, 'I'm a villain, aren't I?' If my son had been there, he would have told this very fine lady to her cringing face that she was a villain and the very devil in flesh. My son, four years of age, knew enough to hate the WestConnex project for poisoning the air and water around his home and digging under people's private properties and releasing toxic gases from the underworld via cracks in the concrete and assembling mounds of odoriferous earth around the houses and the narrow streets and causing the calamitous noise of earthmovers operating at all-hours as they ripped up foundations dormant for decades to make wounds for cement trucks to spew their concrete gush into. All this continuous destruction was daily ringing in the ears of so many good people, who could do nothing but vote Green next election and watch the world outside become obscene to their senses. But what does a four-year-old know? I looked into the dark eyes of that sweet fine lady and swore with all sincerity that she was my new heroine, and I wrote 'God bless you for paving the way to the future' in the little book she asked me to sign, because in those lean days of desperation – for that was the word for it, *desperation* – I didn't care if every animal on earth were tossed two-by-two into the flames. The tropics could turn to barren wastes of bulldozed stumps and upturned stones and all the winding rivers could turn to red-rock desert and the Snowy Mountain Ranges could be flung directly into chasms dug out of the Earth's virgin core for all I cared, so long as the end result saved me fifteen minutes on the morning commute. Those longstanding promises on the billboards over the motorways between the city-proper and the nearest suburbs, the ones promising 'a quicker drive into the city is coming', were as a private covenant from the heavens, and I swore to the lady of the azure gown that I could kiss her on behalf of those whose lot in life was being caught in the livid hell of Sydney traffic.

You-know-who once wrote 'a rose is a rose is a rose is a rose', and though everything else proposed in 'Sacred Emily' has yet to stand the test of time, Stein was right when she put those words together. By some cosmic sophomoric prank, despite my desire to become what some people call a writer, my true occupation on this earth has always been and always will be captured by the construction 'a car-man is a car-man is a car-man is a car-man', and if that formulation makes your skin crawl, *try telling me about it*, since the only escape from this fate of mine is the one Henry Lawson recommended above, and that salvation is forbidden by religion.

According to her own accounts, Mother Teresa was a teacher travelling by train to the Himalayas from Calcutta in 1946 when she heard the 'call' to go back where she had come from and minister to the sickest and poorest souls in that cursed Indian city. As someone who has tried to make a living teaching, I can understand how one might submit to poverty rather than spend another minute dealing with that occupation's horrors, but my own first call to the life of a 'car-man' came to me in my sleep at the turn of the century, in the year 1998, the night after I stood at the top of a cul-de-sac with four friends who had pooled fifty dollars to purchase a car from an enormous man with a wiry beard hanging down to a straining belt. This hirsute behemoth was living out of a caravan on the lawn of a good friend's neighbour, and the car, which was green where it still had paint and decorated by a bucking brumby on the boot, was not worth the fifty bucks we paid for it – the bonnet flipped up and obscured the windscreen as we lurched over a speed hump – and we would have returned it to the man with the beard by crashing it directly through his caravan that very afternoon, but the poor contraption couldn't make its way back up the hill of the cul-de-sac, so we left it there by the roadside at the bottom of the hill, slowly disassembling in the suburban street, until one night it burst into flames and made a lovely light. Next morning, as we made our way to school shouldering our backpacks, the charred wreckage of that dead thing looked like the fossil remnants of an animal conjured up from an underworld, its wheels and windows gone, the road beneath it blackened like an atomic shadow under shards of glass.

During that first short drive where the bonnet had flipped, long before I was granted the right to drive by the state, I first tasted the bitterness of being 'behind the wheel' and had cared for it not at all. Not the clumsy mechanics of the gears, nor the stink of the flatulent exhaust, nor the cramped space of the driver's seat, nor the too-public display of incompetence to which the vehicle's windows exposed its operator. Point of fact, I was so disturbed by this initial taste of motoring I dreamt of doing it again that very night. I dreamt I was back in the car, driving around the streets of my town in the darkness lit by the garish orange streetlights with teenager friends of mine, all laughing and distracting my clumsy attempts to navigate the laneways and hills by turning on the blinkers and honking the horn, while I was busy with the jerk of the clutch and the guys in the backseat stuck gum on my cowlick and yelled out the windows at strangers so that these strangers sometimes chased after us and hurled rocks or shoes at the windows. It was impossible to know, outside of hindsight, that this first nightmare of driving around in a state of alarm and annoyance was a prophecy granted to me from the heavens of my youth-to-be, a time misspent in precisely such activity subsequent to purchasing my first real car, a red and black 1983 Ford Falcon XD, which was 'proud' in the sense that its suspension was demented and its front-end pointed up into the sky while its backside was too low to get over speed humps without crunching against the bitumen, so that it made one feel a little seasick to drive it around in the mornings, picking up my friends for school, inhaling so much Lynx deodorant. As a result of this purchase, I was sentenced to pay for its constant repairs and other myriad expenses by taking work at the Big W in Bonnyrigg, a fate I was fool enough to believe was the lowest depths I'd ever sink to in order to survive in this world whose thirst for petroleum cannot be quenched. And yet, those were the halcyon days, before I really knew how harsh and grinding the road could be, when being trapped in traffic was only a distant idea of someone else's sufferance. Traffic, and its attendant cruelties, was not yet the ever-present doom the wheel of fate was rolling towards my door.

My time as a real 'car-man' began soon after my first divorce, when the car itself became a mobile home of sorts. It was a relief to learn that one could store almost all one's possessions in a Toyota sedan, so long as one didn't own much in the first place and was willing to abandon the few things one still possessed. All your books and clothes and furniture and friends and family, for example, would have to go. But who needs those things when one has a glovebox of one's own, a full tank of gas, an audiobook of 'As You Like It' on compact disc, and some six months' registration? Friends in the mountains took me in after this brief period of destitution, but I was still a parent, and in order to perform those duties I drove down from the mountains to look after my son while my ex worked, so I was forced to face the shuffling halt of the endless traffic laid out like a mass-migration caravan coming down the M4 every morning while the sun rose over the distant city to shine like honeyed amber across the windscreen of the car, making it impossible to see the vehicle ahead until it's within nudging distance. The hard lines around my ever-squinting eyes began to tempt my body with the logic, 'since your lids are almost shut, why not fall asleep at the wheel, ya dummy?' Sometimes tradies, packed into their trucks, wearing yellow vests, their hard hats hanging in the cab, would point and laugh at the dead expression on my face as I slapped my own cheeks to keep awake, or resorted to pinching my arms and knees on the morning drive, or took to playing Einstürzende Neubauten albums at a volume painful to the ears while I passed mocking signs on the side of the highway reading 'How fast are you going now?'

I started to pray away any delays encountered in the two-hour slog past amusement parks and fast-food restaurants and chicken factories and graveyards and abandoned drive-ins and abstract monuments in honour of the charge of the light-horseman and the museums of fire and the lonely bearded men in dirty vests dyed green from the mulch flung up by the mowers they rode along the side of the highway eating up the still wet turf. Stuck in the shuddering, belching, honking wake of traffic, people glance at one another from the private prison of their cars and wonder who among them is the cause of morning radio's petty torments looking up at the mournful face of Triple M's 'Moonman in the Morning' as he watches over us from a billboard constructed where the first suggestion of the city begins at the turn-off to Eastern Creek. There the stench of the eastern tip comes in so strong it turns your stomach, and where Australia's Wonderland once stood, the wooden boards of its rollercoasters crowning into the air like the ruin of a land-locked ark, there is now a set of enormous storage houses for the minutiae of the modern world – the forklifts and pallets and plastic-wrapped cartons and catalogues of industrial activity – displayed in rows as high and long as oil-tankers sitting off the coasts of distant lands, the shining plastic signs announcing the triumph of all this invention bold as a desert sphinx set between the crossing vinyl-black of interwinding motorways. Beyond here lies the real grit of the drive into town – we are only halfway there – at a crossroad offering you the choice of slumming through the grimy car-yard parades between Merrylands and Granville to take the smoke-stained pilgrimage into the choke point of Parramatta Road where it splinters off from the M4, with its smoke stacks and wheat mills and brothels and early-openers and service stations and high-rise developments under construction above the rising roads, or you may circumvent this route by edging your way onto the other motorways that spring from Wallgrove Road, past the smell of rending fat from furnace tops lit like Olympic torches, and curve around old empty fields in halts and jerks, around hills made out of upturned earth topped with barometers and factories named after batteries and bandsaws, until you reach the tunnels into Sydney-town, which spring out under the airport and then sink back underground, with so much of that progress like crawling down the throat of a concrete worm whose oesophagus is serviced by a dead conveyor belt, so the hapless morsels must limp into a digestive tract under the blinking yellow lights encrusted on the grime-grey scales of the tunnel-gullet, each fleshy driver inside these little tin cans staring ahead into the gloom and roar of the tunnel, all their desire intent on being free of their own offering to the city's under-organs, with that silent consolation wriggling in their ears that, once all this creeping and crawling is over with, they can count the hours down until they are regurgitated again, so that all may lay their heads and rest and be on time to re-enact this plaything traffic nightmare in the hours before the dawning dims the starlight in the sky.

Thank God I was not one of those who made their pilgrimage just to work, I was poor but grateful for my unemployment. With my son collected from his home, our mutual obligations to the road could begin, with him safely strapped in back on a blue booster seat, singing songs about bums and farts and atomic bombs, and role-playing games which he insisted must be repeated to the point I could rehearse them in my sleep. 'You work at the police station and I'm going to call you and complain about the movie *Frozen*. Now you are the Chief of Police, and I'm going to call you and complain about the movie *Frozen*. Now you are the Minister for Police and I'm going to call you. Now you are the Prime Minister Tony Abbott and I'm going to call you. Now you are the Barack Obama. Now you are the Queen. Now you are the Peter at the pearly gates, etc'. The two of us would travel back towards the west, going against that still damned flow of morning traffic heading into the city, a pitiable vision on the other side of the streets and highways leading to the house in the suburbs where my aging parents needed assistance with the various duties of life they were now unfit to handle alone – chopping down trees, digging up roots, moving garbage bins overstuffed with garden waste – then we were all back in the car to take the parents shopping in Merrylands to get just the right olives from the deli-markets, or the best fish from the provedores, or the knock-off Autobots from the junk stalls, or whatever desire gripped them that day, and then we would go onto the long flat streets of Doonside to visit the many uncles and aunts, and on to their doctor's appointments in the backstreets of Blacktown, and then back to the local Woolies to be served by the smiling short-haired woman at the check-out, who alone my parents trusted to pack their bags and return their change without some malpractice, and then to Aldi across from the charcoal chicken shops for four-dollar bags of potting mix, and then to Dan Murphy's for three-dollar bottles of shiraz, and then to the golf club to get some discount short-soup and admire the Japanese gardens filled with wandering peacocks just to give 'the boy' some time to run around outside the car with the bonsais and bamboo fountains until it's time to take everyone home, and then rush back to the inner-west to bring my son to his mother's door, and then to hold him goodbye, kiss his cheeks and walk away from that house again like a re-enactment of the original disgrace of leaving, with every street-lamp lining the streets beginning to hum with the hint of evening coming on in its lilac descent upon the city's smoky edges.

It's time to put that all behind me, some voice begins to say, to get back into the Camry with the detritus of the day about you like the moths and cicada songs that enter your room at night, and all your guts are moving out of tune, and you fill up the tank not knowing if you can afford to get home, but it has to run out some day so it's safer not to check how much of nothing is left, just fill up at the one BP station on the corner near the motorway where once you spoke to the guy with the glasses working there and now every time he asks after your wife you say 'she's good', and hope that if you keep the routine up the law of habit will keep the finances secure. The sun is setting in your eyes now, on the windshield like a screen of formaldehyde to keep you fresh for the tomb you're belted into, and it's a funeral march you're engaged in, marching out of the dying city's organs, and the flaring lights of the street begin to shine on every face, the blinking lamps near the motorway give off their indigestions, and now you're back into the traffic shuffle, each traveller on the road with you another coughing private hearse, shadows on every expression like a masking veil, the evening radio sounds ashamed, keeps up a gallows humour, as we slum back past the Moonman's watch, his sagging eyes are now in their full despair and the factory's flames are sombre lanterns over a kind of moving bog of shadows, the bright lights of Parramatta Raceway are swarming with insects and some night-birds are on the wing above the yellowing sky's last light, and our reflections look back at us in rear-view mirrors, red brake lights bobbing and swinging before us on the winding motorway like an eternity of mourners leading candles up the mountainside, and the cold cramp of the coming night and the blue and orange blinking in the windows of the apartments beside the roadside speaks in a kind of electric code. All of this is too much, I know it is, but I was bitter in those days from desperation, and I was in that middle age of innocence where one mistakes complete defeat for losing all, and I thought the life-perpetual of a car-man was the end of hope, never to get back to the beggary of writing proper. The only consolation was my son, waiting for me every morning, a blue-eyed reason for being, though there was one morning, I came to his door and he handed me a portrait of his busy life, aged four, going on five. He had drawn all the attendant characters, his friends and cats and goldfish and so many grandparents the page was crowded with their faces. He pointed to them one by one, announced their names as if I couldn't recognise them, and at last his finger fell on a twisted figure in the background, a man with drooping shoulders and sagging bloodshot eyes, driving a car in a doleful distance from all the rest, stuck on a road with no apparent exit. 'That's you,' he said, and I stood very still in the doorway, holding on to the portrait as though it were the lever of the earth. That evening I drove home the usual way and a storm moved over the night so the moon glowed out behind the thunder like a spill of ink had coloured in the stars, and I saw electric spider-limbs flashing in the clouds all the way up the mountains, trailing an armada of jack-o-lantern traffic in the headlights behind me, heading for that black mountain ahead.

The Writer's Clutter

Vanessa Berry

In the evening when I go walking I can see into the rooms of the houses I pass by. At this time of day the lights are on inside but people have not yet drawn the curtains, providing a view to the rooms within. Sometimes I will see a person sitting hunched over a laptop, but often there is no one and my eyes are free to roam over the details of the interior. The sofas, bookcases and dining tables have the expectant mood of stage sets. Some rooms have a lived-in appearance of disarray, but others are forbiddingly spare and tidy, grey and minimalist.

Give me such a room to write in. Within a week the table will be covered in papers, there will be pictures and notes stuck to the walls, there will be clutter. For I cannot write from anywhere that does not have a measure of disorder about it.

In my own room, my desk is a solid wooden table positioned in a corner, its surface barely visible underneath the sprawl that covers it. Piles of books and papers mound up on the floor around it and threaten to cascade over onto the adjacent bookcases. As is my habit there is an array of pictures blu-tacked onto the wall above the desk. These are postcards and found photographs and other scraps, such as a swatch of a shade of grey paint called 'Secret Passage' and a slip of paper with the saying *patience brings roses* typewritten on it. There is also an envelope commemorating the issue of a French postage stamp featuring Georges Perec. At the corner of the envelope, from inside the crimped borders of the stamp, he keeps watch over me as I sit at the desk.

Perec also preferred his desk to be cluttered 'almost to excess'.

In the essay 'Notes on the Objects to Be Found on My Desk' he examines and categorises the objects which surround him as he writes, observing how they move and accumulate as his work progresses. He lists them and they appear in my mind's eye as if conjured by a snap of the fingers – ashtrays, a bud-vase, a glass full of pencils – some relating directly to the act of writing and others ancillary or talismanic. He notes that this is a sketch towards a proposed larger work, a history of some of these desk objects. They have the power to reveal how the experience of the world arises in ordinary spaces and moments, and how life and the writing of it fit together.

Every day I sit at my desk and look up at the arrangement of pictures on the wall above me. As I work my eyes go up to them persistently, and indeed have done so numerous times as I deliberate over how to describe them most accurately. Found objects, reminders, companions. My attention now lingers over the image of a turtle in a postcard reproduction of a Japanese woodcut. The turtle is suspended by a thin rope, dangling at a window, facing the view of Mount Fuji behind the river in the midground. Sometimes I feel like the turtle. I long to enter the river, but the mountain is the story I must write.

The pictures affixed to the wall are the most ordered part of my writing environment. The desk surface below is an eruption of books, papers, and objects, with a small clear section front and centre at which I sit like a pipe organist, in the thrall of a complex instrument. The collection forms a sympathetic topography, a nest of serendipitous information, in which my own notes are interleaved with items of printed ephemera I've been sent or have bought from second-hand stores. Some directly relate to the work I am doing but others – a souvenir envelope from a dinosaur theme park, and a recipe card picturing a baked catfish on a plate with its mouth open as if about to speak of its woes, to note those which are currently visible – are simply there because I like having them nearby.

In the process of writing, clutter accumulates. A writer's clutter can be physical, like the bundles of papers, notes, and books on my desk. It can be processual: the swarm of edits on the marked-up page of a draft, or the 'offcuts' file of this essay which is longer than the essay itself. It can be digital – a cluttered computer desktop, hundreds of browser bookmarks, accumulations of draft files – or mental, in the psychic turbulence of the process, in the ideas never followed through, in digressions and tangents and distractions.

Clutter can also be thought of as a condition of life. Even the most ordered thinker engages with the complexity of life, and the systems which shape it, when turning to writing. In the work of filtering an immensity of information a writer can only ever create a provisional order with their words. As I sit shuffling the sentences on the page or screen in front of me, it can feel like an act of rearrangement, of structuring an unruly mess.

Spending my working days amid swathes of things that some people would readily sweep into a bin often gives me cause for such reflections. Though I regularly tidy it, the desk and its objects are subject to an entropic force that seems to operate independent of my efforts. This is not something I resent, for my whole life I have tended towards mess. Like the character of Pigpen from Peanuts with his perpetual cloud of dust, objects orbit me. In contrast to the prevailing beliefs about clutter and its stifling effect, this has always been the environment I find most conducive to writing, thinking, and living. At my desk, surrounded by its objects, I can slip into a feeling that I am a thing amid other things, a vessel inside which words gather and disperse.

I am a resolutely analogue writer, and there is nothing I have written that did not begin as a scribbled note on a scrap of paper. Anne Carson describes how there is something 'magically convincing' about the slip of paper which captures the first scrawlings of an idea. Usually for Carson this is the coffee-stained back of an envelope. She continues: 'The same words typed on a nice clean piece of paper wouldn't have whatever it is – fidelity, to your original thought.' For me, this fidelity comes from the particular physical connection of writing by hand. Rather than the rattle of my fingers on the keyboard keeping pace with my thoughts, when I write by hand, I feel thought and word shaping each other carefully.

My equivalents of Carson's envelope are the backs of receipts, paper doilies from under the slices of toast from the Ching Yip Coffee Lounge, pages from the small spiral-bound notebook I keep in the car into which I scribble ideas at the traffic lights, or sometimes the piece of office paper that I keep wedged under the pile of books on the righthand side of my desk – which is ostensibly my to-do list but doubles as a net for stray thoughts. Such scraps are the forest floor of a system of papers, notebooks, and journals that sustain my writing life. The roots of this system are the journals I have kept for as long as I've been a writer, into which I enter the day's presiding details. Then there are exercise books for notes. Spiral bound notebooks for plans. Then the many little scraps of paper, odd-shaped, tea-stained, scribbled-on, that drift across the surface of my desk like thoughts drift through my head.

Perhaps, early on, I supposed I might one day change my ways, begin working neatly, avoid the lure of paper ephemera. But my affinity to mess and clutter runs deeper than an aversion to tidying or conventional systematising or an aesthetic preference. I cannot separate it from the kind of writer that I am.

For all the commonalities within the work of writing, a writer is not a ready-made identity, and there are as many ways of being one as there are forms and styles and voices. Some develop their identity quickly, when there is a situation or idea of such urgency that writing must happen rapidly. For others it is a slower, more deliberate process. For me, whose apprenticeship in writing occurred within the community of zines and underground publishing, before the era of the participatory Web, my development was something of both. I wrote abundantly, energised by a subculture in which writing felt like a direct communication – of moments, of details, of heart – for readers whose lives hovered close to mine. That so much of my writing attained a physical form, printed in limited, photocopied editions, put it in sympathy with the kind of paper ephemera I was given to collecting. I drew strength from writing at the margins, outside of the restrictions of traditional publishing structures, where no feeling or experience was too minor, and no information too obscure, to be of significance or interest.

Around the time I began to take writing seriously I was devoting a similar amount of energy to op-shopping. This was at a time when vintage was still a category for wine rather than clothing, and when the bright 1970s polyester dresses I liked to wear were regarded as an expression of oddity rather than style. Then, as now, op shops were stocked with objects discarded but salvaged, caught between uses, the overflow of a consumer society in which the self can be endlessly remodelled through things. Then, as now, I felt drawn to placing myself among these discards, to search and to salvage. Writing and op-shopping became intertwined activities. I'd sit on a train, travelling through the Sydney suburbs, going as far and visiting as many op shops as it took to unlock my thoughts. Sifting through the objects for ones of interest or resonance was akin to my method of writing. That is, to find within the ordinary matter of life, the details, moments or objects that can speak of deeper things.

To go op-shopping is to surrender to chance, for it is impossible to know exactly what one might find. It was this, underlying the pleasures of searching through the miscellaneous objects, that energised my writing. Along with complexity, chance is also a condition of life. Like fortune, or luck, chance is a way to conceive of forces outside of individual control that shape life in major and minor ways. I still sometimes feel the same existential shiver that would creep over me as a child, when I thought of how readily I might never have existed, if the set of historical and personal circumstances that brought me into being had been even slightly different. Eerie when it comes, always unbidden, is this flash of what it would be like to see back through time with as much clarity as being in present moment.

When I read the Jorge Luis Borges story 'Funes the Memorious' early in my life as a writer, it gave me a sense of what this ability could be like. In the story, after a horse-riding accident, Ireneo Funes developed a perfect, meticulous memory. It was of such power that he could access the entirety of his past experiences with infallible accuracy, and then beyond, seeing into the memories of the things around him. The narrator of the story visits Funes and they spend all night in conversation. He describes Funes's remarkable perception thus: 'We, in a glance, perceive three wine glasses on the table; Funes saw all the shoots, clusters, and grapes of the vine.' This is as much a curse as a gift. When dawn is nearing Funes declares: 'My memory, sir, is like a garbage heap.'

Funes's moods come over me sometimes. The objects surrounding me can be of the grape vine, branching out into tendrils of remembrances and associations. Other times they are of the garbage heap, a glut of stuff amid which I labour. During the times in which I am frustrated with the profusion of things around me, when I stub my toe yet again or some vital slip of paper has disappeared, I turn my thoughts to the presiding, pathological interpretation of clutter that has infiltrated contemporary consciousness: a symptom of malaise, a sign of mental and emotional disarray.

When I identify myself as someone with 'a lot of things', creating and attracting mess and clutter, I can be readily positioned in this pathological spectrum of object relations. Perhaps, in reading this essay, you have located yourself in this spectrum too, and feel an affinity or an opposition to my way of life and working. The restraint of the minimalist grates against the expansive desire of those who favour abundance and the value judgements associated with these identities are powerful social constructs. In examining the figure of the hoarder, Scott Herring uses the term 'material deviance' to describe practices of accumulation that challenge what is perceived as a healthy relationship to objects. By considering deviance we can reflect on this relationship, and what counts as a socially acceptable material life.

The room in which I write pushes at the bounds of acceptability. There's the desk mess, and the piles of books and papers on the floor that often leave only a thin path that cuts across between the door and the desk. I stand back in the doorway, considering the scene, trying to see the room objectively. It doesn't look like the elegant or cosy Writers' Rooms that were featured in the series in *The Guardian* in the late-2000s (except perhaps, that of Russell Hoban, which he describes as dangerous, 'composed of tottering stacks and shaky heaps'). Over the window the broken blind is tied up with a ribbon. The ceiling trails cobwebs that, before the last rental property inspection, I was cautioned to regularly remove.

There is a one-metre-tall, silver-glitter-covered polystyrene teddy bear on top of one of the bookcases, above a shelf of 1960s biscuit tins, in which I store decades of previous rounds of the pictures I've had stuck to the wall above my desk. Below this are the stacks of my journals, the years written onto the spines, arranged in a haphazard order, 2006/2017/1999/2011/2004, and so on down the pile. I often go into them to search for a day or a moment, a process which feels similar to searching through the papers on my desk, or rummaging through objects in an op shop, except this time, the material is my own memory. Every search I make within them, sitting cross-legged on the floor in front of the bookcase, turning through the handwritten pages, I feel the forces of clutter and chance working upon me, pulling me through the thicket of my life story.

So I write in praise of clutter, mess and chance, three defining characteristics of my writing life. The objects that surround me are companions, are an archive, are a manifestation of my way of being and thinking. For I understand my task as a writer to be attentive to life in all of its expressions, material and otherwise, and to find within this the stories I have the potential to tell.

At my desk, sitting amid the ramparts of papers and books,

I turn to the window and look outside. The light is fading from the sky; it's time to go out walking. I push the chair back from the desk, extricating myself from its nest of papers. I put on the coat, green with deep pockets, that hangs on the doorframe, pick up my keys, and set out. The air on this spring night is surprisingly clear and gentle. Birds shrill and streak across the sky. I stand at the gate, deciding which way to turn.

I choose the laneway which runs beside the house, a short, narrow thoroughfare connecting two parallel streets. During the day I look out towards it from where I sit at my desk. Through the gaps in the wooden fence-palings I glimpse the people passing by on their way to the park at the end of the street. Now it is me walking here and I look back over the fence, towards the side of the house. In my rush to leave I must have forgotten to flick the switch. For the window reveals a room in which the light is on but the blinds are not drawn. Inside it there is a view of shelves overcrowded with books and accumulations of decorative objects. In the corner is a desk piled with papers. A chair is pushed back from it, leaving a gap amid the clutter, a space waiting for me to return.

Works Cited

Jorge Luis Borges, *Ficciones,* translated by Anthony Kerrigan et al. (New York: Grove Press, 1962).

Anne Carson, 'Magical thinking.' Interview with Emma Brookes, *The Guardian,* 30 December, 2006.

Scott Herring, *The Hoarders: Material Deviance in Modern American Culture* (Chicago: University of Chicago Press, 2014).

Georges Perec, *Thoughts of Sorts,* translated by David Bellos (Boston: Verba Mundi, 2009).

La Vida

Oliver Mol

1

This is the story of several coincidences, or how I wrote or didn't write my second book, and my hope is that by the end, as in all good stories, we might see literature anew.

2

From June 2017 to May 2019 I worked for Sydney Trains as a train guard, and on my breaks I liked to walk to my favourite restaurants and write or try to write or at least try to sketch the outlines of those stories from the migraine that existed in my head. The work, like most work, was enjoyable and insufferable – but, mostly, I was able to pretend that I was doing something important, something that mattered, or at least something that mattered to me. At Lidcombe, I would walk to that café that sold the five-dollar crabapple sandwiches and try to write about wanting to read but being unable to read; at Campbelltown, I would eat manoosh, or walk to that new café with the four-dollar cheesecake, or, when I had time, eat pho at that Vietnamese restaurant while trying to describe what a ten-month migraine does to a person, and the events that surrounded the afternoon I nearly jumped in front of a train. Occasionally, though, the work became impossible, and I would sit in defeat calling myself a failure until I remembered that I was being paid by the railway, and that the migraine, mostly, was over and that, usually, I could read.

One evening, on my break at Blacktown, I walked to El Jannah and ordered a quarter chicken and chips. It was a Tuesday around

10.30 p.m., and, unable to write, I sat at the last table on the footpath and read from Murakami's *Blind Willow, Sleeping Woman*. The story was called 'Chance Traveller', and Murakami was about to recall a few strange coincidences of his own when I heard an Irish voice and looked up and saw John or a man who I thought was John and his wife walking down the street. John was – is – a writer; in 2015, my first, and his second, book had come out more or less at the same time, although primarily, if memory serves, we knew each other through partying, those fantastic parties Sydney used to have before Covid-19 and before the lockdowns, before we each had our own breakdowns, and John returned to Ireland to work on his family farm. There, he had written *The Cow Book* – a bestseller in Ireland, and a stunning exploration of his own failings and the reparations he had made in his own life; we had not seen each other in four years, and, as I would soon find out, he had returned to Australia, briefly, on a book tour.

John! What the hell are you doing here? I asked, or wanted to ask, although in reality, at least during those first moments, I said nothing; I felt self-conscious, stunned: beyond the greasy chips and dead bird, it seemed unimaginable that this man, this writer, who had proven the possibility of rewriting his own story, would appear, miraculously, out of thin air, and in that moment I recall the unbearable weight and stench of my train uniform, the way it consumed, choked – as if, suddenly, the writer in me were fighting for his life, trying, again, to break free. Eventually, though, I yelled out, John! and he turned, and smiled; he introduced me to his wife. For a while, we spoke: about the book tour, about running, about the world and all the strange and implausible events that had to occur for us to be together, again. Then, towards the end, he said, And what about you? How's your writing going? By then, I had already made the decision to quit the railway and move to Spain, and I lied and told him that the writing was going well, that I was writing a book about the railway, but also about the migraine, and he said, That's brilliant, mate. And do you have an agent? Nah, I said, or tried to say, smiling, almost, because the thought that anyone would want to represent me seemed absurd, and because all I had were these scattered paragraphs written on the backs of train diagrams in pen and pencil that amounted to less than five thousand words. Well, when you have a manuscript why don't you go ahead and send it to me, he said, and we'll see what we can do.

3

It wasn't a few months later, shortly before I quit the railway and moved to Barcelona, that I went to the library in Double Bay and found a book on dreams. I had been having these dreams that were, on reflection, probably nightmares – where trains derailed and doors remained closed and faces appeared to be laughing, although, on closer inspection, were always crying and twisted with pain. The book was called *Why We Dream: The Transformative Power of Our Nightly Journey* by Alice Robb, and when I returned home I placed it on top of my growing, desperate, pile of self-help books next to my bed and forgot it.

But the following day I opened the dreams book and found a bookmark between the pages. On one side of the bookmark read BIBLIOTECA DE CATALUNYA and on the other: BARCELONA. I remember exhaling, looking around, returning to the bookmark, then staring at the flight itinerary to Barcelona I had pinned to my wall. We get it! Sam said, later, when I showed him the bookmark and the dreams book. *You're going to Barcelona!* though, in the end, even he was smiling that bizarre, conspiratorial smile we used to smile as children, back when we believed in mystery and wonder, before we grew up and turned our back on the little people inside us and turned the miraculous away. By then we were at the Eveleigh Hotel, on our third or fourth margarita. I don't remember what we spoke about, but I do remember we had those ridiculous shaved heads that made Sam look like a criminal and me look like an egg; *we need a refresh!* Sam had said, and so we abandoned our hair, but in truth I had wanted to hurt. I was recently single; my actions had caused pain to someone I cared for deeply, and every time I looked in the mirror I saw an ugliness I assured myself I deserved.

Eventually, we stumbled home, but that night, before bed, I remember turning the bookmark over, then over again in my hands, wondering, absurdly, if it meant something, as if I were a character in a detective novel looking for signs, hoping, praying, desperately that something, somewhere, meant something.

4

Then, one afternoon, I discovered I would not receive my visa. There had been a mistake, entirely my own. I had arrived at the Spanish consulate, manila folder under my arm containing police reports, university scores, bank statements, passport and, absurdly, letters of recommendation, and in my best Spanish, I repeated the phrase I had been repeating all morning: *Hola. Yo necisito una visa.* But the man simply replied that, No, they did not dispense visas, that I had to apply online. Later, I learned that the online appointments were booked for the next three months, and that afternoon, in a state of shock then self-loathing then fear, I called my sister and told her that everything was fucked. Who cares! she said. Go for three months, then go somewhere else! But that was the thing I wanted to avoid: the coming and the going, the travelling. I'd been working, travelling on the train for two years and I wanted to put down roots, to stop, rest, pause. I wanted, I realise, now, impossibility: to write a book where, for once, storytelling might mirror reality, and to make this new city that could never be my city my home.

5

In May 2019, I moved to Barcelona, to Raval, to that neighbourhood I was told was a child by day, an adult by night and dead between two and four in the morning. You're in Raval, Robbie would say, eyes raised, with an expression that meant we were no longer children, or that we were no longer in Sydney, let alone Brisbane, and privately I would swallow those words with a mixture of excitement and fear understanding, suddenly, that I no longer knew where or who or what I was.

Throughout that first week, I remember waking early to do push-ups, showering cold, then listening to Rosalia's *Malamente* and *Con Altura*, the music that always seemed to play from the internal courtyard that faced my room. I remember visiting Robbie's workplace, trying to speak Spanish, wishing I spoke more Spanish, filling exercise books with English–Spanish translations, conjugations, then berating myself when I forgot the Spanish immediately. I remember writing or trying to write, though being unable to, walking around those streets that smelled of weed and trash and piss, and those moments my heart beat so rapidly it was all I could do to breathe. Once or twice, I remember walking aimlessly around that bookstore *La Central* and staring at those books by Roberto Bolaño, Valeria Luiselli and Julio Cortázar, reading, briefly, those introductory paragraphs, before calling my sister and trying to pretend I was not in tears. I don't know what I'm doing, I said, or tried to say, because I did not have the words to describe that suddenly it felt insane to be thirty-one, to have quit the railway, to have no plan beyond the vague and fantastic notion of writing a book, or perhaps not insane, but clichéd, pathetic, indulgent, terrifying – because who the fuck was I, I said, to think that I might write something that mattered, to think that I could just pack up and leave and make this new city my own.

6

In the beginning, Robbie insisted on meeting at Barceloneta Beach every morning at 7 a.m. Routine! Robbie would say. That's where it's at, and so each morning, at least during those first few weeks, no matter what time we went to bed, I would run the four or so kilometres to the beach and we would meet and swim and do pull-ups.

How's the writing going? Robbie would ask, sometimes, on the way home, and I would smile and tell him, Not bad, though as the days wore on I would imagine that pathetic, half-sketched character who was not me but who closely resembled me lying on his half-sketched bed holding his half-sketched head and that voice in my head would call me useless, a failure and, while, mostly, on the surface, I would remain enthusiastic, jovial, quietly, underneath, I had begun to occupy a space close to mental paralysis because I did not know how to tell Robbie that I did not know how to build the world that Oliver required – although, after a while, I would simply say that the writing wasn't going, or that I did not know.

Give yourself time, Robbie said, and just relax! But deep down I couldn't relax because without the trains and without writing I knew, or I told myself, that I wasn't anyone or anything at all.

7

Mostly, though, I buried or tried to bury those thoughts, and in the afternoons instead of writing or trying to write I would visit my housemate, Mayte, at her shop, or Robbie and Maddie at their work for lunch, or I would simply walk the streets then return home to lie on my bed or read until the time came to meet Robbie and Juan and Miguel and Marti and Fer and Fanny at Deu Dits, this bouldering gym on the other side of town. It was not the newest gym, nor was it the largest, but it had heart, soul, and we would climb for two or three hours, then do pull-ups and stretch, and each day I felt myself improving, becoming stronger – then one day Robbie said, No more English. No more English, I repeated, nodding, terrified, suddenly, by the prospect of failure, of appearing stupid, of committing forcible mistake after forcible mistake, but after a period of resistance and embarrassment, of stuttering and searching, the bouldering gym became a place of Spanish or broken Spanish and, occasionally, fragmented Catalan, of laughter and inquiry, of learning and play. Vamos bicho! I learned to say, a phrase that means: let's go, bug – one of those Spanish rock climbing phrases that made, and still makes, me want to give up speaking English forever.

8

It's funny – as my Spanish improved, my desire to communicate in English diminished. I enjoyed Spanish sentences, their directness, but more than that I enjoyed the reprieve from my thoughts that anyone can access with only a little commitment to learning another language while refusing to speak their own. Instead of thinking while I spoke – doubting, questioning, celebrating – I found myself simply expressing, or if not expressing then reciting those memorised phrases that kept most conversations afloat, and this holiday from my internal monologue had a profoundly liberating effect on who I was or who I thought I was because like other transformative, although sometimes fleeting, occasionally regrettable experiences in my life – writing, running, performing, climbing, drugs, sex – it made me feel intensely present. Sometimes an idea will visit you, and though you think you have received it, interacted with it, danced with it, you have not, Elizabeth Gilbert says, or I think she says, now, and occasionally, if you are lucky, if the idea feels loved, safe it will even give you a second chance so that its true purpose might be revealed. I wonder, perhaps, if that is happening now, whether this chapter, this essay, is less about language and more about thoughts, that, in the end, I enjoyed talking or trying to talk in Spanish because it allowed me to learn that crucial, wonderful lesson I do not recall learning in school: that we are absolutely, incredibly, not our thoughts.

9

But the writing wasn't going well, and after climbing, after beers and pizza at that restaurant around the corner, after Robbie and I would ride home, yelling, laughing, racing, trying to time those green lights along Carrer d'Alí Bei so that we never had to stop, after we said goodbye I would stay up until two or three or four in the morning, staring at my Word document, listening to those embarrassing, nostalgic songs I would never play to anyone, writing or trying to write, to re-enter the headspace of the migraine, to breathe life into a character very much like myself or the memory or story version of myself, trying to design or recreate a world that I could not see clearly, obscured and warped, occasionally erased, by pain, but trying, anyway, desperately, to guide this character through those sentences, to save him, because, suddenly, again, I had become a god who had trapped a fictional version of himself in a horrible world, and while I had survived, had even rid myself of the migraine, I did not know whether I was strong enough, skilled enough, courageous enough to deliver this character from that invented hell, and that guilt, that inability to perform, to save him, buried me.

Very occasionally, I would think that what I had written was powerful, that I had accurately translated those pictures and scenes from my mind to the page, but mostly I remember feeling so sickened by what I had produced that my neck would seize and the shovel inside my head would once more smash my frontal lobe and I would lie on the floor with my neck supported like I had done all those years ago, and suddenly I would wonder who was trapping who, whether, the fictional me was, instead, trapping the so-called real me, and silently, I would call myself pathetic, and weep.

10

I am going to live or try to live in Spanish, and write in English, I recall writing, once, on some literature residency or grant application that, obviously, was never approved, but in the end, I suppose, the result was the same, and over time I even developed a routine and found several cafés that would allow me to sit in a mixture of self-loathing and occasional surprise with my notebook and laptop in front of me while I drank Vichy Catalan, or green tea, or more commonly beer, and while I was not technically writing, I was moving around paragraphs, occasionally adding and subtracting, and I felt useful, or almost useful, or more importantly, surrounded by people, less alone. In the end, though, the only café I went to was on the corner of Carrer dels Tallers and Carrer de les Ramelleres, where I abandoned that migraine book and began writing those fictional stories that I would never show anyone, and at the end of each day I would throw those papers, gleefully, dramatically, in the bin. But what is the point of writing if all you do is destroy it? Maddie asked, one evening, at Bar Brutal. I don't know, I said, honestly, although perhaps, in hindsight, I do know: because what interests me, now, about this rather banal memory, this almost masochistic display of destruction, is not that I would abandon story, but that I would abandon outcome, that I would focus on process, that instead of improving my stories I was learning or relearning to love the mechanical, the physical, what that eminent Australian architect Richard Leplastrier calls: the relentless pursuit of pure purpose – that the point of a story might have less or nothing to do with story, but more or everything to do with the pen, and the way, occasionally, it might suspend thought when racing through a sentence, a paragraph, like this one, before stopping, briefly, at each full stop.

Course, at the time, I wasn't thinking about any of that; I was simply pretending, I told myself, to be a writer with the vague hope that one day that fiction might become true.

11

One afternoon, after a day of writing sentences only to delete them, I closed that blank document and went for a run. I ran harder than usual; I was angry, or I was scared, and I sprinted, almost comically, until I could no longer breathe. At some point, I called Sam and told him that I missed him, Sydney, our friends. I thought I would make friends instantly, I said, suddenly aware how pathetic I sounded. And I have made friends, but – and then I told him I missed being hugged, kissed, touched. I confessed, as if it were something to be ashamed of, that I had not been touched, properly touched, by anyone since I arrived. Maybe this is a period of not being touched, Sam said, and then, in that higher octave, in that octave where I could see his smile, Maybe this is a period of learning to touch yourself.

It's comical, almost, now, to pause, to return and acknowledge those jokes told by friends that, in the end, were never jokes at all – because, of course, there is that wonderful and terrible metaphor that writing, and especially the writing of ourselves or the translated versions of ourselves, is masturbation, that it is indulgent, frowned upon – that if we absolutely must it should be done quickly, in private, then locked away or hidden, like in a journal, and never spoken about again. But masturbation, as it turns out, and despite the rhetoric learned from parents or media or church or school, is not evil but a form of self-love where, away from screens, we might connect to our breath and settle into a state of flow where we lose sight of goals and distractions and simply reward ourselves for being who we are. To write, then, or to practise writing well, is to unlearn certain perfectionist, goal-orientated behaviours we learned from adolescence, and to be with ourselves for lengthy periods of time, strictly, in discipline, in compassion, in exploration, in kindness.

But, at the time, it was not funny, and I remember smiling, or almost smiling, trying to smile. Besides, Sam said. Of course you can't make close friends straight away. Those take time, but Papi – give yourself a break! You're in Barcelona! Soak it up! Treat yourself to some tapas and sangria! Sangria's not the problem, I said, my voice cracking, then hating myself for it. I just – I can't – I don't know how to write.

12

I've quit writing, I told my sister one afternoon, and to her credit she accepted that lie with grace and compassion, and even congratulated me for it. And, for a while, even, that lie became truth, and instead of writing I walked around museums and galleries, or I hiked up Tibidabo, or I simply rode my bicycle through various neighbourhoods listening to music. Once, I caught the train to Tarragona because I thought, or I thought I had read, that Bolaño had lived in Tarragona, but he had lived in Barcelona, and then Blanes, and so, instead, I stared at that second-century Roman amphitheatre; I drank vermouth; I walked along the beach and sat on the beach and watched people play in the water.

It's just hard, I told Maddie, another night while staring at my negroni. What's hard? she asked. I don't know, I said, immediately feeling pathetic – and then, for the next hour, I rambled on about wanting, but not having a mentor, or a boss, or security, or a clear path, although, in the end, all I communicated was that I was scared, that I had a problem believing in myself. You know, Maddie said, as we were leaving, if you can't write about the migraine, why don't you write about that? About what? About believing in yourself.

13

Another night I returned home from climbing and Mayte was having a girl's night; everyone was drunk and laughing and I wanted to be drunk and laughing too. For a while, I stood there waiting to be invited, but I wasn't invited. So I said, Have a good night! and returned to my room. Then, absurdly, I burst into tears. But these weren't normal tears. These were heaving, inconsolable tears. Irrational – absolutely, but that's how it was. I think, deep down, I knew that I had always distracted myself from writing about the migraine through friends and drugs and alcohol, and suddenly, in that room, I knew there was no one to blame for my inability to produce but myself.

At some point, there was a knock on the door. I remember my stomach, the way it knotted, suddenly, with fear: they had heard me wailing, I was sure of it, and I began wiping my eyes, trying to erase that private world that I did not want anyone to see. But in the end it was just Mayte's friend, the one I had a vague crush on, wondering whether I had any weed. Oh yeah, I said, staring at the floor, but then she said, Hey, are you okay? and before I knew it, I was crying again. I felt ashamed, embarrassed – I still do – I did not know how to articulate my problems to myself, let alone a stranger, and I wished, rather melodramatically, to disappear. But then, after I gave her the weed, she asked if I wanted to join them, and even though I declined, finally, I smiled because the image of myself trying to explain to a group of girls that I had been crying because I could not write seemed absurd, and because, suddenly, I remembered that quote by Scott McClanahan that I still think about more than all the others, that quote I would trade all the words I have ever written to have written: I knew he believed in something that none of us ever do anymore. He believed in the nastiest word in the world. He believed in KINDNESS. Please tell me you remember kindness. Please tell me you remember kindness and joy, you cool motherfuckers.

14

Life, I suppose, unlike a story, or a certain kind of story, is not plotted, and scenes, even those memorable ones, are forgotten, although occasionally they resurface, and after another day of not writing at that café on the corner of Carrer dels Tallers and Carrer de les Ramelleres, I returned home and buried my face beneath my pillow. I wanted to scream but I could not scream; I did not want anyone to know or hear and I did not want to put anyone out. So I punched myself in the bladder. Then I did it again. Then I wrapped my hands around my throat and choked myself until I couldn't breathe. For a while, I lay in the heat. At some point, I slept, and when I woke from that horrible dream I decided to read. I was rereading Bolaño's *Last Evenings On Earth*, that text I had fallen in love with all those years ago, and that, inside, on the front cover, I had written: *this holds the key to something*, but I couldn't find it; my bag was too full, so I turned it upside down. There, amongst old notes, books and pens was the bookmark from my dreams book, and for a while I stared at those words: BIBLIOTECA DE CATALUNYA wondering, suddenly, where that library was. So I typed the name of the library into Google Maps and a short, blue path appeared. I walked from my bedroom to the living room and stared over the balcony. The library from my dreams book was right across the road.

15

I remember, that afternoon, walking slowly towards the library, under that archway that Danny would later be robbed of his gold chain, then staring, in suspicion, in hope, at its façade, and that building that had once been the former Hospital de la Santa Creu but was now a home for books, and allowing myself, briefly, the metaphor that even the most rigid structures could change. But when I tried to enter I was unable to; I did not have a library card, and could not get one, so instead I sat outside the library and read 'The Last Evenings On Earth', that story that gave the book its title, a story so sparse, so beautiful, that, even now, when I read it, I still become hopelessly, dizzyingly, lost. But, halfway through, I grew tired; the heat was unbearable, and my head began to burn, but I couldn't go home, not yet, not after the punching, the choking, so instead I returned to the café on Carrer dels Tallers and Carrer de les Ramelleres and ordered a beer and thought about all the stupid and fucked up decisions I'd ever made. I thought how I'd been a train guard once but was a train guard no more and how I would never have that security again. I thought how I'd hurt the person I'd cared for the most and I deserved to be alone and I deserved pain. I couldn't write and I would never be able to write and that invisible me deserved to be trapped in that horrific labyrinth from which the visible me could only watch, while offering no way out.

How do we talk about those miracles that haunt, that take us outside ourselves and allow us, however briefly, to believe in the world again? At some point, drinking another beer, staring idly at 'The Last Evenings On Earth' I began to wonder where Bolaño had lived in Barcelona, and where he wrote. Eventually, I found an article in *El Pais* that said Bolaño had lived in Raval: *en el numero 45 de la Calle Tallers*, and then, in another article titled 'The Wild Side of Barcelona Literature' the author claimed Bolaño had frequented the bar on the corner of Ramalleres, 27, and in something between shock and incredulity and awe, I showed the barman the article and the directions and asked where they were and he smiled and pointed around us and said, Aqui. For a moment, I couldn't move, could only stare; then he took my arm and outside, around a corner I had never bothered to look, he pointed to a plaque that read: En aquesta casa va viure l'elscriptor i poeta Roberto Bolaño, and finally, I exhaled – for a moment, through the window, I stared at those tables, and, briefly, in secret, allowed myself a fragment, an alternate narrative where I dared to imagine Bolaño and I sharing the same seat, writing or trying to write, inside.

That afternoon, after I got home, I told Mayte about the bookmark in my dreams book and the library across the road. I told her how every day I wrote at the same café, and out of all the cafés in Barcelona it was the same café that Bolaño had written at, and that he had lived in the apartment above. I told her I didn't believe in much in this world, but I did believe in stories – even those broken, fragmented ones. I told her storytelling was time travel, and then I looked away and allowed myself, once more, that dream where Bolaño's ghost and I sat next to one another and the world felt less alone. And then, finally, I asked her if she thought it meant something. I wanted to tell her but didn't tell her about the paralysis I felt in front of the page, the screen; I wanted to tell her but didn't tell her about that hatred, deep hatred, I felt when I couldn't produce. I wanted, in the end, hope – to know whether she thought I was crazy, whether, in the absence of so-called *real* support or mentors it might be possible to raise those literary heroes from the dead.

Of course, Mayte said, her eyes wide, and then, with her hand on my arm, Don't you see? It means *everything*.

16

Listen: this story could be told a million different ways; it could even be a happy story, the story where a character moves to Barcelona for three months and flirts with Spanish before continuing his travels elsewhere, but this isn't that story, this is that private story, that hidden story, that story we falsify and distort, hoping, praying, it will never be seen.

Here are some quick, happy stories: I remember on that first, or second, outdoor climbing trip staring up at the cliff face while Juan patted his dog, Boston, and Robbie and Marti spoke: about the climb, or about their lives, or about the future of graphic design or literature or magazines, although, in truth, I do not remember what they spoke about, only the *way* they spoke – with such directness and sincerity and humour and conviction, and I felt, perhaps, for the first time, that these were men I could learn from, that, one day, I might even talk to others and myself like that, and I knew if I ever wrote about Spain, I would write about that moment, and the way, lead-climbing outdoors for the first time, they yelled encouragement as I attempted, though failed, to clip my rope through the next draw, and as my arms and legs shook, as I yelled, Tension, or, I'm going to fall, Juan yelled, Te tengo, that uncommon phrase that means, I have you, and I fell two or three metres before stopping, suspended, in golden light, above the forest or almost forest floor.

And I remember the day after arriving to Barcelona piling into a rental car with Robbie and Marti and Clemente and driving to the

Pyrenees and hiking, gloriously, on snow shoes, for hours until we arrived at the refugio that we had, by luck, entirely to ourselves, and as the sun went down I remember feeling so jet-lagged and tired but also, positively, absolutely, alive and later, by candlelight, we ate dried meats and cheese and perhaps, though I cannot recall, even some wine, and eventually, after talking for several hours, Robbie said, Tell them some stories, and I played Seekae and Nils Frahm and Thomas Gray & Liam Ebbs – those musicians I am writing and even listening to now – while I told those stories about the migraine I had performed in Sydney only several days earlier, and Clemente put his hand on my shoulder and told me, a stranger, That really touched me, and Robbie said, Yeah boy, smiling, and before bed, unable or barely able to keep my eyes open, Clemente said that he wanted to take a photo.

17

Ottessa Moshfegh in a recent interview with *Apartmento*: My relationship to creativity is that I always want to feel creative and I always want to be having fun with it, but I'm not always able to do that. So I hang in there for what feels like really hard work, because it is, and I earn myself ten minutes of ecstatic creativity after maybe eight hours, and then in hindsight it's all been fun, but it hasn't always been easy.

I love this quote – because it's true, and because it exemplifies the importance of ritual, process, and brings to mind that wonderful and clichéd metaphor of a climber not staring at the peak of a mountain but at their shoes, trusting in their footsteps, sentences, paragraphs, fragments – because of course this essay was supposed to be different. In the beginning, I had planned to write something about creativity, or my growing understanding of creativity, or about certain problems I faced while writing or trying to write, or about certain authors and people I learned from, or about what it meant to no longer have a migraine and to be able to write, or about how I quit the railway and left Australia and spent my life savings, absurdly, trying to write a book – and I had even written or tried to write myself letters full of anti-perfectionist reminders and Julia Cameron and Elizabeth Gilbert quotes and advice from those future conversations with Sam when, still working on that book and paralysed by fear, he told me that he had experienced those same terrifying seeds of doubt while working on his second album, but that all I had to do was get out of my head and return to my heart – you need to turn off the thinking, he said, and you need to return to a place of trust and love, and then he told me that we were going to create a mantra. He said, Every time your head says you can't do something, you're going to repeat: I am doubling down on myself, and then he told me he wanted me to write it out. He said I was to put that phrase next to my computer and every time I stopped working because of fear I would turn those words into a roar – because here's what you have to remember, he said, finally: all the skills you have learned while practising your craft have got you to this point, and those skills, if you trust and believe in them, will continue not only to hold you, but your work will expand and grow and end up in places more interesting and unexpected than you could have ever dreamed – and I had even planned to send that letter, really send it with an address to myself in the past in the hopes that it might turn into a prayer or a sign or many signs, because I wanted, finally, to love myself, to give myself or the story version of myself, at least in literature, an assurance that everything would be okay, that Tim O'Brien had been right: that storytelling was alchemy and time travel was real, but in the end, this essay, this story, had other ideas.

18

One afternoon, in a state of unbridled optimism, I organised a reading in Madrid, and the following week I packed my bag and rode my bike towards the train station at Barcelona-Sants. I remember a light breeze, listening to Princess Nokia and pedalling between large groups of people, finally able to relax, as if I were on a holiday, which, even though I rejected that term, I suppose, I was. I remember, on the train, reading Alejandro Zambra's *Not To Read*, and stumbling across his essay on Natalia Ginzburg whose *Family Lexicon* I had read in Sydney, and had left me unable to think about much else for weeks. At times he was very unhappy, Ginzburg wrote about her friend the poet Cesare Pavese, but for a long time we thought that he would be cured of this unhappiness when he decided to become an adult; his unhappiness seemed like that of a boy – the absent-minded, voluptuous melancholy of a boy who has not yet got his feet on the ground and who lives in the sterile, solitary world of his dreams. I recall, absurdly, turning that sentence over, then over in my head, staring at countryside, wondering, melodramatically, whether Ginzburg had written those words for lost boys like me.

In the end, Robbie and Mariana came to Madrid; six people attended the reading, and afterwards Robbie said, I really liked it. I thanked him, although in truth I felt embarrassed – these were private, sketched or mostly sketched stories about the migraine I had written prior to Barcelona; I had performed them to people before, and they had responded with laughter and tears, and I wanted, more than anything, to move Robbie too. I looked up to him, and I wanted him to feel what I felt and to see what I saw; I wanted, if only briefly, for him to hurt, to smile, to understand, even a little, because, maybe, then, ludicrously, I would feel like what I was doing mattered, that what I was doing was not as wild and stupid as the voices told me, and perhaps, if only for a second, I would feel that I mattered too. This, of course, is preposterous, and later, in therapy, a psychologist would simply correct me and say: you seek validation from others while never giving it to yourself.

Later that night, at the Mexican bar, we had a fight. The particulars do not matter. The fight, like all fights, had little to do with one another, and more to do with ourselves.

19

And so I embarked on an unbearable two-week trip through Cordoba, Seville, Granada and Málaga. I was to leave Spain soon, and thought travel might fill the void left by literature, but in the end it was a disaster. Mostly all I remember was that horrific flamenco show in a cave where the performers were hungover, or still drunk, and American families kept yelling, Cerveza! and Bueno; the Russian mother and her thirty-year-old son who stayed up all night drinking vodka whispering, laughing, then whispering and yelling at one another from opposing beds; that girl who was crying inconsolably from her top bunk in the middle of the room. Robbie had lent me *Johnno* by David Malouf, and later I returned to the room because I wanted to read it at dinner, but when I turned to leave she apologised, and told me she was stressed. I'm so stressed! she said, and then she explained she was trying to write her masters thesis from this shitty, fucking dorm room. Fuck this dorm room, and fuck this heat! But, in the end, we went to dinner and she explained she was from Valencia, and that her life was in shambles. No really, she said. My boyfriend and I broke up several months ago; I'm finishing my thesis in a hostel dorm room; I'm smoking too many cigarettes, but at least I'm able to express my emotions. In any case, I'm over Spanish men. They're romantic, but they're all babies looking for a mother. And you, she said. What are you here for? Holiday? No, I told her, but then, before I realised, I was babbling about love or loss or loneliness, or about how people in Australia, or at least the people I knew, got fucked up and fucked, to which she said: of course you feel lonely – you're in a place you know nothing about. Besides, all you foreigners think Spain is one big orgy. But we are deeply conservative: mostly, all the partying and fucking is done by all you *guiris – que dices! Que va!* I said, and for a while we laughed. But then she said, You didn't answer my question. Why are you here? I'm not sure, I said, finally. I guess I'm trying to write something, but I don't know how. The answer sounded as pathetic and cliché as it reads now, but she considered my answer, then said, Well, if you're a writer, and you can't write, maybe you should visit the house owned by the late poet Federico García Lorca.

20

Ever since I was left somewhat alone, without gods, I have been a ferocious believer in the power of small coincidences, says the writer Valeria Luiselli, and the following day, on the way to Lorca's house, I kept, silently, repeating his name. I kept recalling, repeating his name the way a person too important and beyond the scope of this story had, months earlier, before Spain, when we were in love or almost in love, before I fucked up and everything went to hell. I kept hearing her voice, her poetry, seeing the night she had said: Lorca visits me in my dreams, and when we arrived my breath cut short and I held it because I still had not forgiven myself, and I wanted to hurt. That afternoon, accompanied by a friend from the hostel, I walked around that poet's house, and staring at that painting on the wall by Salvador Dalí I saw the night she had told me Dalí and Lorca used to be lovers, and from that memory burst other memories, and by the time we arrived at his desk I knew that if something didn't change soon I would disappear. My friend, to her credit, must have known something was wrong, but instead of inquiring, she just nudged me and said, Pretty good desk. I bet even *I* could write a masterpiece here. What sort of masterpiece would you write? I'm not sure, she said, or I think she said, or I imagine she said, now. Probably something like *Back to the Future,* but with more romance – one of those stupid, literary stories where the characters attempt to fix their problems by travelling back in time.

21

This story should end here: with the protagonist apologising, once more, or better: with the protagonist, finally, forgiving himself, or best: with the protagonist picking up a few of those self-help books and learning to say I love you so that he might really hear it and learn to say it back – but now it seems clear that this story was never about the protagonist, that, in the end, he was no more than a secondary character in a larger narrative about second chances: a courier or vessel, briefly, for certain ideas before they returned, rightfully, home.

Shortly before leaving the poet's house we visited the gift shop and I purchased Lorca's *Romancero Gitano*: a present for Mayte to say thank you for allowing me to live in her home. Along with Robbie, she had made my transition to Barcelona incalculably easier, and I wanted to give her something that let her know I appreciated what she had done. But several days later, when I returned to Barcelona and gave her the book, she let out a deep, resounding, Noooooooooo. Oliver, she said. Are you fucking kidding me? Then she told me an ex-boyfriend had gifted her a copy of that book, but after a fight she had thrown it out the window in a fit of rage. I never saw that book again, she said, although I thought about it often. I thought about it so much because I wanted it to come back but I knew I could never buy it. I always wanted to read that book, to know it, to apologise, and now you have brought that book home.

But now it was my turn to go silent – because several days earlier I had written a note on the front page, a note I would like you to read now:

Dear Mayte,
This book is for you. I searched long and hard through Madrid, Cordoba, Granada, but it was, on my final day, that I found this book and it seemed to be screaming for you. We were at the poet's house on a tour – perhaps it was the colour of the cover – who knows – but I knew it was for you. Sometimes, you just know.
Love
Oliver Mol
4/7/2019

22

Here's the truth: I do not believe that the world is fated, but sometimes a series of events will transpire in such a way that it is hard not to believe in a God, or the universe, or something large and invisible suddenly revealing itself, as if to say that the purpose of the essay and life were the same: that our only objective is firmly, and with great attention, to continue; to kindly, sincerely, *try*.

Perhaps it's best to end like this: Sometimes, or often, it's only in hindsight that we recognise certain paragraphs are meant for certain texts. There are essays, such as this one, where paragraphs written years ago are finally able to fit into a space, to come beautifully, gleefully, home. So, perhaps, now I write not for outcome or meaning or purpose, but for them: for those long, lost paragraphs that are waiting, finally, to come home.

Subject Line: The Storyteller

Lauren Carroll Harris

The email arrived on the day that rent was due. Subject line: *The Storyteller*, from a man whose job title was 'digital recruitment consultant'. 'Friday tomorrow, happy days!' wrote Caleb. He'd found me on LinkedIn, and said he could connect me to some potential short-term contract work, if I was open to it.

I was open to it. Surviving as a freelancer is like chasing a sheet of sand. After the end of my PhD scholarship – really, a form of writer's welfare – one job offer evaporated after the other. I was headhunted for what was ostensibly a dream job – in actuality, a succession of two short contracts at a failing magazine. A high-paying job at a media organisation was informally offered. A contract was promised but never appeared. I ran the treadmill of casual academia, attending the two-hour lectures without pay in order to tick my students off on the roll. My flatmate moved out and I became an AirBnb slumlord to pay the remainder of the rent. I picked up casual marking work at other universities and speed-marked assignments at a rate of three essays per hour.

Underemployment is stupid-making, costly and time consuming. Each day I woke up with the goal of earning $150. I should have been working shifts at the local bar. Instead, I was turning around arts stories within a day for $140. I was the equivalent of an Uber driver for freelance-dependent media organisations – available and on-call for the smallest bite of work, bringing my own infrastructure and capital (laptop, internet connection, phone) to the outsourced workplace of my home office. I invoiced supposedly liberal outlets for poverty pay. I invoiced the public broadcaster for joke money. In the gig economy, this intricate piecemeal hustle – what Jan Breman has called the work of 'wage hunters and gatherers' – is celebrated by many as entrepreneurial gusto. The same people would argue that the only thing worse than working is not working. Or, in my case, not working enough at the right things. Without a boss, I was what philosopher Byung-Chul Han calls a self-exploiter: a journalistic auto-bot toiling for my own failing enterprise.

'My client was voted in the Top 5 of Australia's Best Companies to Work for in 2017, need I say more? Either way I will...' wrote Caleb. 'This will be 2/3 days per week over a 4–6 week period and is paying around $350 per day, so it could be a nice little earner on the side for you. I'm looking for somebody who loves and has a flair for Storytelling, an eye for detail and the ability to sift through copious amounts of info!'

I called Caleb to thank him for this great opportunity. 'Happy Thursday!' he said. I pictured a white guy leaning back in his office chair, hands stretched behind his head, talking via Bluetooth. The job sounded sweet: over ten days, I would prepare the client company's submission document for its formal recognition as one of the Best Places to Work in Australia. Great Place to Work®, I was told, is a vibrant industry leader and a global authority in workplace culture that compiles a yearly list of Best Places to Work. To attract the best and brightest talent, the local branch of a transnational IT company wanted a place on that list. They needed a researcher to collate policy information, staff testimonies and workplace successes in a neat and tidy story of employee satisfaction.

I was introduced via videolink to Anya, my future manager. Though she was based in the communications department of the company's Bangalore office, she was making a brief trip to Sydney that would coincide with my first days. She sure was looking forward to partnering with me on the project.

The document I was to produce would comprise ten chapters responding to the Great Places to Work criteria – recruitment, workplace culture, philanthropy and other *actionable insights*. Anya suggested a starting point. I should meet with the SMEs. What is an SME, I asked via email. 'Subject matter experts,' came the one-sentence reply. 'Sent from my iPhone.'

HR showed me to my desk. Ian, a user-interface designer seated next to me, put out his hand to shake mine. 'You're a new team member?!' he asked. 'Oh no,' I jovially adopted my most enthusiastically ironic tone. 'I'm just here short-term. I'm an intruder!'

His double-take made me realise the error of my approach to throwaway office banter. A social imperative was already exerting itself, one more conducive to dull inquisitions about weekend activities than ironic quips. 'I'm working on the "Great Places to Work" project for a couple of weeks.' Ian's face relaxed into an expression of understanding. Ah, yes. Language that could be comprehended. By the end of my time here, I came to understand what this narrowly salvaged interaction meant: I wasn't a good *cultural fit*.

I began to schedule interviews with the SMEs. I listened, and transcribed their experiences of working at the company, what drew them to the company, how they felt about their aspirations, their experience being 'onboarded', whether they felt they were being developed and valued. A set of familiar phrases began to recur in the transcripts. We're a family here. We're a thirty-year-old start-up. We're for the little guy. We bring our entire selves to work. I put my journalistic training into gear and tried to find the local angle, rephrasing questions to trigger responses that I hadn't already heard. It was no good. There was no cutting through the company line. We're powering prosperity! We're *all about* giving back. Philanthropy is *who we are.*

Anya's idea of what made the company great to work for was imitation Nespresso coffee pods and foosball battles in the office. Parental leave, even if your child is adopted. A relatable, approachable leadership team that exemplified the company's friendly flexibility. The fact that one of the Sydney executives lived not in the bourgeois Eastern suburbs but in the more bohemian Inner West. She left the office at 3 p.m. each day in time for school pick-up, and resumed working from home after 7.30 p.m. once her children were in bed. What time did she finish work, I wondered? Once a year, she would rough it overnight in the CBD in a sleeping bag as part of the CEO Sleepout. She put her money where her mouth was and struck the ideal work/life balance. Work/life balance was important to the company, which was made of team members, not staff or employees.

On my second day, a message from Anya menaced my eye in Slack, the great interrupter. She said there was a 'town hall' – companyspeak for staff meeting – at 1.30 p.m. It would truly be a great opportunity for me to see the company's great team dynamics and transparent leadership style in action. I made my way downstairs to find that most of the seats were already taken. I edged in and found an empty seat next to a young-ish guy with a glossy, beautified beard. I could see Anya in the row in front, a few seats to my left. There was some small, funny, foreign object bearing the company logo on my seat, and I absentmindedly put it on the floor beneath me. The crowd of a hundred or so team members was watching a stadium-style address streamed from the company's headquarters in California. On the screen, an executive was maniacally roaming a stage, equipped with a headset microphone, his forehead glowing with sweat. He was gearing up, he said, to let us in on a big announcement, but first he had to reinforce something. He paused and put a finger in the air. 'We are laser focused on our customers. We live and breathe innovation, and champion those who dare to dream.' The bearded guy next to me leant back just a tiny bit, blinked, slackened his mouth and nodded slowly with comprehension and admiration at this moment. The executive continued. 'And now, before I let you in on this secret, you gotta promise – nobody tweet this! Nobody tweet what I'm about to say! This is legit confidential, okay, you got it?!' I treated myself to a sneaky glance at Anya, who was smiling and looking over at her colleague next to her with a gasping expression of astonishment at the Twitter joke.

'Here it is, folks. We've just hit *one...million...customers!'* The screen cut to a screaming headline, ONE MILLION CUSTOMERS. Clip-art confetti fell for a few seconds. The team members around me jumped up from their seats, trembling with corporate lifeforce. They cried out in joy and rapture. I became aware of a most peculiar, most stressful sound of the type that cannot be produced by a human body. I looked around, to realise that the implement I had removed from my chair and placed on the ground was a mini hand clapper – three plastic hands, imprinted with the company logo, that smacked together to produce an unnaturally loud form of applause. Anya was wildly flinging her clapper back and forth, her arm and chin held high, her eyes shining demonically with pride and shared achievement.

—

'Capitalism begins not with the offer of work, but with the imperative to earn a living,' wrote Michael Denning in his essay 'Wageless Life'. You don't have to be working for Deliveroo to be a gig economy worker. More than ever, for those of us locked out of permanent jobs, work is not the way to wealth. It keeps us in poverty. Work is increasingly about sending and receiving emails, or worse, Slack messages. Few political parties speak seriously of the idea of full employment, the cornerstone of the Australian government's economic policy from World War II until 1975. Anybody who wished for a full-time job could find one. Full employment is a decision; providing employment is a governmental obligation. Now, the employment contract has melted. Unemployment – and underemployment, my scrambling fate – is a failure of the economy.

During my commutes home from the company, I began to notice an old school friend pop up in my Instagram feed. I remembered her as my birthday twin. She had moved to Texas at the beginning of high school for her dad's new job. Her photos now revealed the life of a Texan homemaker who had taken her husband's surname. One picture showed the sign to her residence in an estate called 'The Colony'. She was pregnant with her second child, and taking a steady stream of shots of her craft projects and family meal plans. 'Finally put together a bow holder!' enthused a typical post, with a picture of a repurposed photo frame that displayed her daughter's hair ribbons. 'Such an easy DIY with a frame, ribbon and hot glue #diy'. The world had spun us into different continents, different lives – evidently different value systems – and yet we were both spending our days drawn into useless, underpaid or unpaid busy work.

Women's domestic labour, work in the arts, caring for those with illnesses and disabilities; scratching life, wasted worried workless dispossessed life. There I was, a drifting leaf in the metropole, floating across the categories of employed, self-employed and unemployed. I pictured myself as a leaf often. On the bus to the city, I would think, 'Who would want to be a person in this scene? I'd rather be a stone, or a bee, or a leaf.' This slipperiness of identity is something I've come to embrace. Identity categories are my terror. I'm a blurry person, able to adapt to many scenarios (well, except a lifetime of office culture), and that's enough for me. My own identity, and knowing what that is, is less important than being known by a few people who are important to me.

But back then, nobody knew me, and I didn't feel cared for. I imagined that everyone around me at the company had something to earn money for: doing a little job and living a little life to serve a mortgage, a growing family, a partner, some kind of honourable purpose for sacrifice and money-making in an economy of belonging. I was alone, unit-less, and learning that partnering and inheritance was how individuals build wealth in this society. Gig life is the new master trope of my generation.

So I sent Anya a first draft of the submission. 'A few red flags,' she replied from Bangalore, along with the marked-up document. By this stage, I had worked for free on the project's preparation ahead of being in the office, and was working longer days. I wasn't scheduled to work more that week, but Anya asked me to go into the office the following afternoon to revise one of the sections. Pathetically, obediently, I complied.

The red flags that Anya spoke of were, namely, that the document needed a greater focus on the company's core values. I went back into the trove of internal documents to see what those core beliefs were and how I might better represent them. One of the tenets, I learned, was a heady devotion to customer satisfaction. 'We fall in love with our customers' problems,' I wrote as a subheading above an employee's reflection on selling the correct software to a client who teaches dance classes in the suburbs. 'We deliver unrivalled customer benefits to power their prosperity. We sweat every detail of the experience to deliver excellence.' I found another core value I had not adequately reflected in my prose: 'We Care And Give Back.' 'We are stewards of the future,' I wrote in a new subheading, reworking the Corporate Responsibility report from the previous financial year. 'We strengthen the communities around us. We strive to give everyone the opportunity to prosper.' But surely these milquetoast mantras weren't what the Great Places to Work assessors were really looking for.

Early the following week, I completed my timesheet. More than half the allotted days of the contract had passed. Not long after, Anya queried why I had logged the impromptu afternoon from the previous week in my timesheet. 'Oh, when you asked me to go into the office? Those are the hours I worked,' I emailed back.

I went downstairs to the food court, found a seat in the corner and waited for Lex, a friend who was also working in the city, albeit on a much more lucrative contract writing copy for a company that sold lavish overseas holiday packages in *exotic* locales to wealthy baby boomers. Our lunches and post-work meet-ups were mutually miserable. 'It sounds like your daily rate is a scam,' said Lex, almost completely without affect. 'If they were paying you an hourly rate, you'd be earning almost twice as much.'

We were in one of the newer, space-aged food courts, fitted with high windows, grass-fed burger franchises, poke bowl vendors and millennial-friendly climbing plants of the kind that are popular on Instagram. I should sell out completely instead of doing this halfway bullshit, I thought. Looking around at men in business shirts slurping laksas and gesticulating to one another, I realised: these people are on a track. They have jobs in sales and marketing. They have mortgages. They get promotions and bonuses. They hit their monthly targets. They have furniture loans. They have car loans. They go to Friday afternoon drinks. They evade *the missus* and then placate her with flowers and chocolates. They are on a path, I realised. They are Part of Society. Only apparitional me lived and thrived among them.

The daily rate is a scam, I thought.

—

There were early signs in my life that I was less than equipped for the corporate world. At age fifteen, I found myself in need of something more than pocket money. A friend was a manager at KFC in the city. The trouble started on training day, when my manager friend passed around tiny lapel buttons with a 2D blocky person, rendered in a red and blue colour scheme. A small but assertive speech bubble escaped the valiant worker's mouth: 'YES!' At KFC, my manager friend explained, we were *yes people*. On my first shift, a customer came up to me while I was mopping the floor and asked me if this was my first day on the job. I lasted four days. Weeks later, my paycheck arrived: $77.

Fifteen years later, and ten years after the Great Recession, as the GFC is called overseas, the gig economy was booming. Work was everywhere! But the very notion of a job, with a workplace, employer, union, salary and benefits had disintegrated. This time, when the chance to join corporate society came sliding into my emails, I thought, 'I'm adaptable, I'm a twenty-first century person.' But still I was not a yes person. I was a sullen, shocked teenager again, thrown into pure Freudian regression by the gig economy's latest insult to my low-rent dignity. *God forbid I die in Australia*, I kept thinking, at my temporary desk at the company.

I opened a new Slack window and explained to Anya that we would need to rethink the timeline, as there was no way that all ten, thousand-word chapters of the Great Places to Work submission could be completed within the ten-day timeframe. Was there any possibility to extend the contract?

I watched the ellipsis as Anya typed, and I waited, and I played it cool. 'That's all the time we have Lauren. And we've to do the best we can,' she replied in the chat window. 'It may not be absolutely perfect but we need to be able to close this. I know you are used to interviewing celebrities. How can I help you to work faster?'

She was a robot. I was 'in the churn all day' in Lex's words: working ten or eleven-hour days, typing mercilessly, running to the bathroom when absolutely necessary, skipping coffee breaks. I didn't have the smarts or savvy to come up with a suitable answer in mystical companyspeak to Anya's question. This is a confronting thing for an intelligent person to learn about themselves: that they don't have the presence of mind to respond in the way that is needed to a given situation. And I was in a situation. I simply wasn't ready to combat whatever deeply transactional, passive-aggressive managerial techniques that Anya had weaponised. That night, I Googled 'management techniques how can I help you to work faster' and found a story on *Harvard Business Review* on how to get employees to work faster. The post was tagged 'developing employees'.

I emailed HR and asked for a meeting. 'It's become apparent to me,' I explained to Jane, the HR officer, 'that the timeline and the workload don't seem to have much to do with one another. Now I've gotten a handle on the role, it seems to be more of a twenty-day task than a ten-day contract.' I told Jane about how Anya had admonished me for logging all my work hours, and the fateful half-day that she had tried to extract from me, a non-employee, as a freebie.

Jane was great at performing empathy, and therefore, great at her job. She listened the hell out of me. From her, I picked up a new term: 'capacity', as in, 'I'm at capacity', which I was. Jane told me the duration of the contract had been decided according to the budget that was available; ten days of payment were all that the relevant department wanted to account for in the budget. There was a reason, I came to understand, why the company's marketing staff hadn't been assigned the Great Places to Work submission; everyone needs skilled writers, but nobody wants to pay properly for them. I was learning in real time that writers' abilities are indispensable. To analyse, to conceptualise, to quantify, to qualify, to describe, to enliven, to narrativise – these are not necessarily the tasks of marketing and communications staff, nor could they be performed, for this role, by the tech company's software engineers, programmers and designers. They are the skills of a writer.

However, Jane said, carefully and non-specifically, no contractor is expected to work more than seven hours and forty minutes per day. Afterwards, I dopily realised nothing had been promised or acted upon, and nothing was communicated between HR and Anya. I also realised that the document I was preparing, and the internal reports I had been drawing statistics and information from, spoke only of the company's benefits for full-time permanent employees, and said nothing of the engagements or provisions of contractors. Nothing people, untethered, uncounted. No superannuation, no workplace entitlements.

Caleb called, zealous, upbeat. 'Hey hey Lauren, happy hump day! Just a quick call to see how the job's going, as your contract is approaching its end!' I explained to him what I explained to HR. 'Ah, I see, I see,' he hummed and mmm-ed. I explained that Anya had objected to the way in which I had been correctly logging my hours. By this stage, she was emailing me at 4 a.m. Bangalore time, broadcasting the kind of ostentatiously inappropriate hours of a manager who wants her underlings to know how hard she's working and expects the same. Caleb sent me a follow-up email: 'Just try to do what you can in the time you have left and don't worry too much about it for now.' Smiley face.

You may think I'm being hyperbolic. Maybe I am, I don't know anymore. Is it melodramatic to say that the gig economy doesn't care if you live or die?

What is it to earn a living? What would it mean for your contribution to be valued? How would it feel to be certain of your worth? And of the jobs available, how many advance your prospects, and how many are useful to society?

I emailed Anya that I had prepared the document to the best of my ability within the timeframe. The chapters were in a perfectly decent form. Shaped, edited, copy-edited and proofed, punctuated with photos I'd sourced of team members delivering food to the poor as part of charity programs – but not highly polished. I would be available to respond to further edits and feedback if the budget was there to support that, and I would be leaving at 5 p.m. Anya did not reply.

I lay down for a while, preparing to slink back to my freelance journalism efforts, and delayed getting a bartending job once again. I began to stop striving. Started floating. The next year, the company was listed as a Great Place to Work.

Five Ways

Miro Bilbrough

Every technology offers gain and loss. This is my accounting, a personal arithmetic of screens and apps engaged with over one, exceptional year.

1. Face Control

In what quickly established itself as an everyday routine on desktop camera, Zoom kept my thoughts from the horror of the unfamiliar virus engulfing the familiar world. Zoom saved my job as a casual teacher of screenwriting during Lockdown.

In between Zoom appointments I took modest walks where I savoured most things.

Crystalline atmosphere and absence of fire smoke. (It was mid-2020.)

Berms no longer summer-singed yellow and brown.

Beds of reeds my whippet yearned to get lost in.

A cactus tree that made the turn into a particular dead end worthwhile.

Stuffed bears in windows and trussed to fences that wore out their welcome but stayed put anyway, depilating with the months and turning to cliché.

It was so quiet.

Two children homeschooling in a downstairs rental who had taped their paintings to the French doors.

How did I know the terrace was a rental?

I don't know. I just did.

Each day I made sure to induct myself back into the

non-pixelated real via those slow, suburban square dances, circumscribed in the days of the five-kilometre radius and threatened number plate checks, but off screen! Off-screen in all senses, *in* the senses.

Even so, by the end of that year of social distancing and technology getting-closer, my face felt so exhausted, held so tight, I felt it might slide off. Or maybe I just wished it to. Teaching a miniaturised humanity as frightened and disoriented as myself who preferred not or, for reasons of bandwidth, were unable to switch on their cameras; mouthing at black squares instead, compulsively checking my enfeebled smile; astonished and embarrassed by the depressed but camera-friendly complexions of youth; the Zoom grimace of the one nominally in charge (me) day in and day out. This was how I spent the greater part of the first plague year, 2020: in a state of urgent calm.

I have read that the babies of mothers with post-natal depression are often unusually animated, facially expressive: an evolutionary ploy to capture their mother's attention. In a reverse of our chronological ages, my students had become a proliferation of emotionally remote mothers (and fathers) and I, running the gamut of micro expressions, a rubbery visaged infant who couldn't capture their attention. A grotesque analogy, but so was the situation.

Right before he turned off his camera, one production student said to his roommate, *that really sucked*. I thought so too. He had laughed through most of the workshop with his off-camera other in a way that made it clear that they were watching another screen. Even so, of a dozen or so students, he was one of only three who had bothered to make himself visible, to turn his camera on. Maybe he was referring to that salient fact. During second semester I had not and would not meet one of the new university students on my screen in the flesh.

I was unconvinced by online learning, but we all knew why we were there. To hold hands digitally through a terrifying historical moment that stretched on and on. There was the student in Minnesota, hastily restored from Sydney to the family home, who never missed a class even though it was midnight his time. Gareth was a digital enthusiast with beautiful manners who looked more and more wan as Lockdown stretched on. I made a point of asking him how it was going in his city each week, and he, of minimising the distress. Pretty soon only his sister was going out to procure essentials and we stopped talking about it. I figured he needed an hour of escape, to take his mind off the burgeoning unknowns and self-begetting sameness, just as we all did. Like most of my students he was back at home, returned to a childhood he had only just left. There weren't sentences to contain all this on Zoom, and even if there were I couldn't elicit them. I tried to remember the validity of simply being there while fencing heinous levels of Imposter Syndrome. Sometimes this worked, when I showed up in the Zoom 'breakout rooms', Gareth was a shining light of participation. His passion seemed part native and partly an outcome of living under palpably higher stakes than most Australians.

By our final hour of the semester, a pedagogic intimacy had taken shallow root. Of a class of twenty-six only six turned up but everyone had a script idea to talk about, five had their cameras on, and only one had a failing connection that kept him stumbling in and out all class. My own image got darker and darker as daylight closed. It was winter and my lamp cast a poor sidelight. I was a filmmaker in need of a gaffer, or to reframe what I *actually* was these days: a casual tutor of screenwriting who hadn't sorted her lighting. I got up to turn on the main light and returned to my only marginally better lit square. It was satisfying work because their script ideas had become, finally, articulate and quite suddenly these screenwriters actively sought my expertise. Useful at last! I had only ever met them as animate postage stamps and I would never see them again, but at 5.50 p.m. on Thursday, Week 11, the Zoom room was warm. We were going to miss the weekly assignation I had come to dread.

Right before we signed off my eye flicked to frame right and there, on my closed wardrobe door, hung a bra of the most transparent lace. A cartoon signifier of, well, a bra. Setting up, I had tilted the frame upwards to a position immaculate of bedroom furniture but a last-minute costume change, followed by a nudge of the laptop when I reached to adjust the lamp and – here was my bra. I surveyed five sets of eyes. All lowered to their scripts. I told myself no one had noticed. That if they had that this was a souvenir of Zoom akin to the child in a tutu who crossed unobserved behind an older-brother student at his desk and, later, back again, absorbed in her sweetly purposeful domestic business plunging those of us that noticed, unbeknownst, deeper into the incongruity of the Zoom Dream: a realm that is strictly business, but which can trip the passive observer into the unfiltered and private without warning.

—

By the time I was back in a staff room, I found I was not alone. There were others chewing the inside of their cheeks at night, busy making scar tissue that hung conveniently low to be re-gnawed, or breaking molars from clenching and grinding (I was a grinder), checking our plague privilege then going to bed to clench and grind or chew again. Nocturnal bruxism is a 'parafunctional activity', apparently, which I take to mean pointless but not meaningless. Bruxism escalated during Covid as we parried fear by day, passing it around like the object in a dread game of pass the parcel. By night the parcel landed, and we locked it firmly in our jaws. Michi, a cinematography teacher, had discovered a pressure point that acted as an 'off switch' accessed from inside the mouth at the back of her jaw. I could never find it. I practised licking my lips, clockwise then anticlockwise when no one was looking, unconsciously replicating my whippet Nestor's gesture when nervous. *Lick-lipping*, apt that it is a tongue twister.

This year, Zoom has been replaced by commutes on trains, by lecturing in rooms or consulting in an ex-sound recording room that is no longer hermetically sealed – it leaks sound – and whose walls are battered by acting students doing warm-ups and vocalisations across or down the corridor.

Fuck you Fuck you Fuck you!

No Fuck *you* Fuck *you* Fuck *you!*

My face has not forgotten. It continues to hold on for dear life (life is dear) and I don't know how to make it stop. I blame the technology of screens and its proliferation. I blame Zoom for scraping my job off the Lockdown floor and, here's the catch, reconstituting it on a small screen that has turned into more screens. Everywhere, screens.

Irena, a psychotherapist, recently told me that bruxism is a concentration of energies that we express and circulate as we move through the day. At night, in the physical stasis of sleep, this energy lacks the release of movement and concentrates fear, anger and other unexpelled emotions in the jaw. This simplest but most organic of explanations has helped more than magnesium supplements, mouth guards or going to sleep with my tongue between my teeth as if wedging open a door. Irena's offering feels apt because it fits with a sensation of outrage, deep seated in the body, that so much time spent at screens is suppressing the expressive language of our bodies.

Since talking to Irena, I get up and write or drink tea in the kitchen when I wake in the night. Just that tiny bit of movement seems to help. On those occasions I am less likely to awaken with the woozy face ache that is the legacy of 2020.

2. iPhone Hieronymus

I am straining to enlarge tiny figures in a Hieronymus Bosch painting with the two-digit splay that I have thought of as squirrelly since I first became conscious of train carloads of commuters doing that and the swipe circa 2016. After a shuttered morning spent in three live screenwriting tutorials, I hold the device inches from my masked face. The essay's writing and its projection into the visual have a trance-like clarity. Against the wonder of the fifteenth-century painter and admiration for his twenty-first century critic, however, I feel the physical pressure of narrowing and loading my focus into this flat, radiant, tyrant of a space. It is tiring being wet tissue to a screen. That makes me sound like a mussel; a muscle attached to a machine.

The phone battery, set to Low Power Mode, is down in the teens. Enough.

Exhausted, my eye passes effortlessly through the carriage window and along a ramp-like road into the shadowy balconies of sandstone-storied Central station's upper eastern façade. If you were writing this for a moving camera, the movement would be one very long tracking movement or dolly, although this would fail to capture the full *sweep* of the thing as the gaze becomes aerial. But I am out of date, my technology is as rusty as my directing – a drone could do this.

The journey of my naked eye in this sudden, deep perspective is like a sigh or an exhalation, a kinaesthetic empathy for the unfurling of the climbing road to Central station. Unleashed from the suspended time-space of a very small screen, I experience a minor ecstasy of the real and of real time. Ah, movement again. Ecstasy for the Ancient Greeks was 'to stand outside oneself'.

A life lived via screens is a generator of great emotional and physiological tension, of suffering even. And yet. Refreshed by my recent drift, I am free to...look down at my phone again. At a detail of a jester hunched over his cup in the fork of a tree in Bosch's *Ship of Fools* (c. 1505–15). There's something about the jester's outfit. Are these light-beaded outer layers transparent or threadbare, T.J. Clark wonders:

> *Dazzling as they are, [they] don't seem to be deployed just to dazzle. I think they're meant to float the figure into a realm of fragility, vulnerability even pathos – anyway, somewhere different from the idiocy below.*

For a moment that's what I am, bedazzled, floating, fragile, as technology unfolds the magical, the human on a homebound train.

3. Transitions

Sometimes when a film student fails to show up with a script to a one-on-one consult, I get lucky. The student doesn't have a story idea yet but is thinking about screen language. *That* is their idea and so we talk about editing or camera technique and I remember that once upon a time I was a filmmaker. Even better, that technology can be a vehicle for creative thinking.

The students sometimes bring me golden thoughts, ideas not quite clean of psychology – which, as we know, can get surprisingly trite – but almost.

Jack wants to discuss transitions. The way you can be watching a close-up of a character, studying their expression, then there is a cut to a wider shot and you find that the location has changed. The character is no longer where you thought they were but somewhere different. The filmmaker has seamlessly transported you through time and space in an unusually disruptive way. Perhaps the stealthy relocation signifies a dream leap or thought jump, a psychological effect, after all. Perhaps it indicates genre, a thriller or crime story that keeps you, the audience, running to catch up. Sidestepping expectations of continuity editing, a time-space paradox ensnares the viewer. You feel disoriented and quickened.

Niall doesn't have a script either but comes armed with that rarer thing, an aural imagination. Is this why he tends to look Off rather than make too much direct eye contact – Off as in off-screen, although he has the pallor of a night owl, too – as if he is listening to peripheral frequencies?

It is to Niall I owe the journey back to Thomas Edison and earlier for, in the small hours of the night, he has come across the inventor's voice recording from 1927. This was thought to be the first of its kind for the longest time until, in 2008, a lab in California restored a man's voice singing the nursery song *Au Clair de la Lune* from a 'waveshape on stoveblacked paper' made and patented in 1860. *A waveshape on stoveblacked paper?* A kind of sound drawing, then.

Frenchman Édouard-Léon Scott de Martinville's goal was to make 'daguerrotypes of sound'. Niall had been listening to the result, lost to history for only a hundred and fifty years. He tells me he prefers the uncleaned-up 'original' version, wavery and at the wrong speed, which makes the voice sound eerily feminine, semi-submerged in noise. A mushroom-like glow concentrates his face as he attempts to capture the moving effect this voice from another time had on him. He looks off to the side, smiles, shakes his head, smiles again.

When I track down Scott's recording its effect is overshadowed by my experience of Niall's face listening in recollection. 'He had a great show on his face', the infant daughter of a flatmate once reported back from her day at preschool of another child. Impressed by her linguistic insight at the time, today I can find no other way to put it better.

4. WindowSwap

Sunday morning, I prefer to be at Lina's in Ramallah, where the view opens onto a building-encrusted hill: mid-century apartment towers gentled by uniformity of ivory palette; at hill's crest the more ancient shapes of distant spire tips; in the foreground a scattering of birds taking off from, circling and landing on a house. With instinctual good taste they have chosen the one fanciful piece of architecture available – pagoda rooftops, a covered balcony, two satellite dishes, a geometry that refuses symmetry. The sky is faintly overcast.

I can visit Lina's thanks to WindowSwap, a website comprised of the pre-recorded views of contributors from around the world, launched as a quarantine project by Sonali Ranjit and Vaishnav Balasubramaniam in Singapore.

I detect Lina's presence, standing at about the same point I am sitting in relation to the screen as she subtly reframes, nudging a grey moiré curtain, unsettled by the breeze, further into view in her apartment. It is moving to be in Ramallah at 6.22 on a Sydney morning even though I cannot tell what time it was for Lina at the time she stood there, steadying her horizontal phone to record her view, in a territory that has imposed on it a different kind of perpetual, cruelly involuntary lockdown.

After a while, I realise I have been listening to roosters, muffled by glass. It is early, then. While I am writing this a musical horn surprises me. A quick harp strum. My ear tells me it belongs to a bus, but I cannot find one on any of the three roads that snake in and out of Lina's view behind the buildings, and on which a man in a black thawb strode earlier. It is just as Walter Murch suggests, off-screen sound can trigger a subliminal perception of worlds and plots unfolding beyond the limited film frame, an effect the sound designer likens to the 'kind of thickness a novel gives off'.

The vistas uploaded with recorded sound certainly offer the deepest perspectives, the more literally transporting affect. When I flick back between screen windows to check a detail, the sky over Lina's has cleared, is luminous and high. I leave the view to its own devices to describe it instead but keep an ear on its aural business. The constant dull traffic is like the roar of the sea in a shell.

The view out my window is comprised of potscrubber trees above a lichen-tiled roof; stands of olives and lemon trees planted as a 'functional garden' by our landlords, the Jabbours, who grew up in this building and who were clearly thinking of an earlier home in the Lebanon hills; pink ombré suffusing to palest blue as I write.

The day in Ramallah has aged. The sky, looking less new, more seen-it-all-before, tells me so. Here, too. I hear Nestor's exclamatory toenails on the kitchen lino. In a second, he will pass me on the way to the yard. It's breakfast hour. The view cycles to the next window. The ten minutes of the website's allotted timespan are up – more, because I kept returning, could not go past Lina's, perpetually re-unfolding in real time even though that time is long past.

5. Russian Nights

But Face Control, I first encountered the phrase after midnight in the backstreets of St Petersburg, down towards the river, when it had at last fallen dark. It was 2005. The club was nothing much plus a bouncer on the door, a brutalist archetype who I watched refuse a young local. Hanging back, a small group of us set up shop on a couple of crates outside. A middle-aged Russian scholar with the wily build of a wit and an extremely tall, young American post-grad in tow to prove it, explained that this was Face Control at work. If you were judged attractive you got in. Not, not. The American who was collecting stencil graffiti for his American supervisor and writing about electrical motif and metaphor in early modern literature for the Russian, got in. That he was beautiful was beside the point. He was male. He was American. Inside, a couple of low-ceilinged rooms throbbed with smoke, death metal and dim. He came straight back out. Outside was where it was happening.

One glimpse was enough to convince me of my solidarity, to return outside where the scholar and his acolytes drank warm beer from plastic cups. We fell into a conversation about *Days of Eclipse* (1988), a film tinted with irradiated yellow light, made by Aleksandr Sokurov before he got famous for his much lesser, one-shot hit *Russian Ark* (2002). Set in Turkmenistan, I'd seen *Dni Zatminya,* as it is called in its mother tongue, at the Chauvel sometime in the nineties. I might as well have stumbled upon a piece of asteroid in the streets of Paddington. The scholar quizzed me about why I liked Sokurov's lesser-known film. I muttered something about tobacco filters...like a yellowed daguerreotype...and the slippery consciousness of the filmmaker as his narrative melted distinctions between the real and magical with such casual unaccountability, such oblique can-do. I loved films like that. Still do. Even so, I felt self-conscious extolling a Russian film to a Russian scholar, and annoyed that he sat back so comfortably in the power relation. I kept up a good face (another kind of face) while despising my reflexive desire to please. The scholar remained tacit, gnomic even. Maybe the whole world was his student.

—

Earlier, on the Moscow International Film Festival's opening night party barge on the Volga, I had witnessed Face Control in action without knowing its name. There I observed that whatever the code was it did not apply to the bloated grey flesh of organised crime persons who appeared to double as festival friends and patrons but that it did apply to a fellow filmmaker. Georgina was a first generation Mexican-American from Arizona who was later to take out a big narrative prize at the film festival, one of the only non-Russians to do so. I took her exclusion by the forbidding blokes on the door as racism pure and simple. The sexism was so intrinsic it passed, as it so often does, without comment.

I hadn't met her yet but after that night, Georgina and I fell in with each other in the way of travellers in a city where the Cyrillic street signs never became less foreign. I quickly discovered she shared my family disposition for moaning, a tendency that was at first startlingly exotic – the freedom to moan so much!, almost Chekovian in this geographical context – as we tooled around, peevish with jet-lag, giant floating pollen and White Nights, on barges and through vegetable markets thronged with gold tooth grins. Outgunned, I no longer had the desire to complain and, besides, I was having too good a time looking at everything. Georgina's verbal fretting finally became too circular, fixated on a film program curator, a bespectacled Muscovite in a boxy short shirt (everything about him ironically square) who had offered to take her around but kept cancelling, further inciting her speculative romantic attachment. We discussed our mutual failing and she confided that everyone in her large matriarchal family moaned. Her movie was like this too, she said. About nothing but full of people talking and moaning.

That's one of my definitions of art, made of overlooked materials, right under the nose of the everyday. The non-celluloid moaning, however, was the making then breaking of our too-quickly plucked friendship that, like the fruit of the aphorism, spoiled fast.

That night on the docked barge I whipped in to see what I could find to eat and to take back out. There was a second barge, well stocked with vodka but little else, on which the festival hosted the opening night reception for the filmmakers and where the Mexican-American returned to wait out this hungry, estranging night in the rain. The other barge, I discovered, was a fairytale scenario: trestle tables with engraved silver samovars served tea but were otherwise laden with empty bread baskets, dishes that bore the scud marks of dips or had been licked clean of caviar, and platters piled high with chicken bones. It was as if I had strayed into the den of ogres, of short, wide, suited men who had done their work in the company of the 'Night Butterflies': statuesque blondes with strapped-on trays of Smirnoff. It was a venal enchantment.

As for Georgina, the curator finally came through and we parted company on Tverskaya Street. She was off to rendezvous at the Yeliseyevsky store. We had wandered its aisles of unalloyed imperial glamour just that morning and came dully out with a tin of tuna each and handfuls of beautifully appointed Turkish sweets made of shitty compound chocolate. Now she was going back there to meet him, the promise of another party in the air in the company of this elusive debonair wafting her spirits.

I never got to see Georgina Garcia Reidel's *How the Garcia Girls Spent their Summer* (2004), but I last saw the filmmaker with her suitcase in the reception of the Green Apple Hotel. The curator was there too, poised to drive her to the airport. She looked fluffed, replete and, despite so recently finding we didn't get on, I found I was pleased for her happiness. We smiled at each other, a quick exchange of regretful self-knowledge, and didn't speak.

Unearthing the festival catalogue, searching for a face, a name, a title, I find that her film:

explores the terrain of longing, loneliness, and self-realisation among three generations of single women in a Mexican-American family as they struggle with lack of romantic exercise.

It is the sardonic 'lack of romantic exercise' that gets me.

—

In the Petersburg alley the scholar was hatching a plan to take us to see Palace Bridge raise itself up and split into two halves so that ships might pass under along the Neva between 3 and 4 a.m. and asked me along.

The group was comprised of the two American friends, Max, an autodidact theorist of tragedy interning at the film festival to improve his Russian, and post-grad Ben. Plus, a local girl Max was tutoring in English, and her buddies, passing a bottle of warm champagne to celebrate high school graduation and keen to kick on to another death metal club that might let them in.

I have since regretted that, glimpsing that elusive destination Sleep, I went back to my hotel bed instead where, after having passed the execrable Face Control and done absolutely nothing with it, having blagged my way through the alley-way oral exam, I failed to sleep once more.

Like the flatmate vampires in Taika Waititi's *What We Do in the Shadows* (2014) who find themselves able to watch the sunrise on YouTube and not suffer the consequences, I have since visited the famous foot and traffic bridge, lit violet and underscored by Russian consonants and tourist din, opening online. Unlike the vampires, I would rather have seen it in the flesh.

Works Cited

T.J. Clark, 'Aboutness', *London Review of Books*, Vol. 43, No. 7, 1 April 2021.

Michael Ondaatje, *The Conversations: Walter Murch and the Art of Editing Film*, Bloomsbury: 2002.

Fight or Flight

Lisa Fuller

The cursor blinks.

The perfect horror of the blank screen stares back. An eel curls and bites my innards. The urge to run is strong.

I place my fingers on the keys. Hot sticky blood beneath the nails.

This isn't supposed to be how it is. I'm supposed to be enjoying it. Chasing the dream.

Maybe if it came easy, like it seems to for everyone else. Like the first book. *Ghost Bird*. The one that only a short six months ago was thrown into the world carrying my hopes on its slim spine. I told myself, it's only a debut, just the beginning of my journey as a writer. Tempered my expectations. The eternal pessimist, always hoping for the best, planning for the worst. I miss the characters. I want to find their voices again, throw them into hell and watch them overcome it. Then came the shortlisting, once, twice, three times! God, the excitement and the absolute terror. How am I ever going to top this?

Trapped inside my house, I exist in multiple worlds at once: the shocked writer with the shortlisted first book; the absent academic with the unfinished manuscript; the aunty who reads her latest manuscript to her nieces and nephews every night, and revels in their excitement. I feel trapped in a wave-tossed dinghy: Can I write? No, I can't! Maybe I can? No wonder I feel nauseous.

I want to whack my head against the wall. The first book wasn't easy. It took me a decade of hard work, feedback, rewriting. Somehow in the retelling I make it all sound so minimal. I take a breath. Tell myself I should be proud of my efforts.

But writing *Ghost Bird* can't have been as hard as this?

I'm sure I didn't come away from each writing session feeling like I'd damaged myself. And why? Is it too close? Too real? Second-bookitis? This time not witnessed from across the safe distance of my editor's desk? I empathised so much with the writers I worked with, but it's a whole new ball game feeling this firsthand. I can't rationalise it away.

Does this new work just suck? The last three attempts at a second book sure did, each one tried and abandoned at different points. Fifteen thousand words of one work here, 45,000 words of another there, the half-chewed corpses litter my computer files. None of it good enough. This attempt will probably be the same.

I battle on. There are moments of flow, where I lose myself in the story, the characters – their voices take over. Joy racing my fingers across the board as they struggle and fail to keep up with my thoughts. So many missed words. Typos.

Urgh, you're an editor dammit! If you can't make it good, then at least make it clean.

And there she is. My dark passenger, so good at disguising herself as me. I lean back, reaching my hands behind my head and tip my face to the ceiling. Trying to stretch the tension from my neck and shoulders. I'd kill for a distraction, an excuse to run.

My mind grasps the email I received last night from a creative writing student. A student who appeared so confident in class, yet here they were asking me for help, outlining all their fears. All refrains I have seen or heard from myself and my students before. None of them are unique – but this is the first student I've had be so open and honest about their feelings. I admire that bravery, that vulnerability, and my heart aches for them. They say they can't write, that their dream is pointless because their writing sucks, how their marks never match their hopes or expectations, confirming all of the above. They're drowning too. God, can I relate. I didn't know what to say. I mulled it over the whole night – how to help them when I can't help myself? Admonished myself for opening work emails at 10 p.m.

This morning I'd sent off the longest email that I've ever written to a student. I told them straight, there are no easy answers. I'm struggling with all these feelings myself – imposter, fraud, bad writer, worse person. That these feelings are normal, and they are not alone. I never had high marks in my creative writing classes at university either, but we all have to start somewhere. They're only in their first semesters: try to be patient and learn as much as possible. No one goes to a couple of art classes and expects to paint like Monet. I encouraged them to join a writers group, to seek out like-minded passionate people. Find interviews or pieces by their favourite creatives speaking about how they handle this. Try their strategies and see what happens. Because there is no 'one way'. No magical recipe for how to address these feelings. Only the way or ways that will work for them.

I should keep a mirror on my desk, take some of my own damn advice.

I told them to understand that writing is a practical task, one that often gets underestimated. No one can pick up a book and see the years and years of hard work and multiple people who worked on it – so we assume it came into the world looking like that. The only way through is never to stop writing or learning. I'd sat there staring at the screen for a long time before I forced myself to hit send. I only hope it helped.

I wish we could have had this conversation in class! Guaranteed all of my students are experiencing some version of these fears. It could've helped all of them. I miss their faces, their voices. The discussions and disagreements that technology just cannot compensate for. Seeing lightbulbs go on as things become heated or hilarious. Watching all of the interactions or exercises spark something creative and inspiring in a person. That human connection.

The last sentence of the email read: 'I need to print this email out and hang it above my desk.'

And here I sit. No printing done. No writing done. Staring up at the ceiling looking for ways to run from my writing. Keeping my mind off my students, and my favourite line to them – Just write!

I yank myself away from my desk. There's only so long I can take my own bullshit before I get annoyed.

I have two options. I can sit here and push through, or I can get into the shower. Ignore my work for one more hour. Then another. Maybe do some chores. The kitchen is disgusting.

Does it have to be either/or?

I step under the spray, draw the steam into my lungs. Heat slices my skin, warming my bones and loosening aching muscles. I take a seat. The country kid in me is horrified by the waste.

I close my eyes. Imagine that inner voice, sitting opposite me. The tough, mouthy teenager with defences too high for anyone to scale. She's wary and angry with me for putting us in this position. I've always admired her will and speed with a comeback. She's the protector. And tormentor. Because to be safe, we must never risk.

Never be vulnerable.

I look beneath her, like the counsellor showed me. To the scared little girl buried inside. The one who'd been so out of place, bullied by teachers and children. For being Blak but not Blak enough, smart but not smart enough. The Teen grew up and protected the Kid. I can't help but feel proud of her. But now we're all scared.

Scared that we're not good enough to have our dream.

Scared what we'll show if we are.

Each publication has brought a fresh hell of inadequacy. Awkward realisations that I've revealed too much, buried in conversations with readers.

Failure was never a word we were allowed to own. Now we have no control of it. And to fail at this one thing, that means the most?

In her young face I see my nieces and nephews. I know this age. God, poor kid.

I extend my arms and pull the Kid in for a hug. Forcing the Teen to come too.

I've given this to everyone but myself. I don't want to be the tortured writer who never finds their way. I want to write, and share. Embrace joy. And risk.

We vow to find the fun. Together.

Stepping out of the shower, I prop open the window. The steam rolls away from it. Feeling the chill, rain-soaked air on my skin, racing over me in a pleasurable way. Dressing, I try to keep the calm close. Hold it in like a breath I'm scared to release.

I pad over wood floors to the makeshift lounge in our renovator's delight. Soon the walls and ceiling will collapse under the hammer. I find my nest. A single spot on the couch, filled with notepads, laptop, diary, knitting, throw (last year's project), phone, charger, handbag, random things and cushions to sit on and support my back. The white and pink dog blanket laid out for the needy staffy who camps beside me, occasionally shoving her large square head in front of the keyboard, or pushing the laptop oh so slowly off to one side. Spoilt little goofball.

It is always a nest, but right now it's a rat's nest. As is my office space. My partner despairs, unclear why I can't bring myself to work over at my desk. I'm not sure either. It's better over there – no TV, no knitting, not as many distractions.

I sit and type and let it come.

The words flow now, not fast, but they're moving. I want to clean up my couch-nest, clean the desk, and find a rhythm, a pattern that serves me better. Distraction? No, stay here and write!

The Teen and the Kid wait. They're still there, staring out through my eyes. A habit of a lifetime can't be broken that easily. But they've always been there, and I wrote a whole book. And I'm still writing now.

Trapped in Negation

James Ley

A couple of years ago, I was working as a sessional teacher at a university when management handed down a new decree: from now on all employees must undergo a 'working with children' check. This struck me as odd. While I don't discount the possibility that an institution of higher learning might have to accommodate the occasional underage prodigy, university students tend to be high-school graduates, which means that even the freshest fresher will usually be at least seventeen. True, this does not technically qualify someone as an adult, but a seventeen-year-old is not exactly a child. More to the point, I had been hired at short notice to teach a course for second- and third-year students, none of whom could be mistaken for children.

The university management, in other words, wanted me to jump through a clearly inapplicable bureaucratic hoop. They wanted me to prove I was a respectable person with no criminal past that might make it risky for them to place children under my care, so I could walk into a classroom full of adults the following week and discuss an Angela Carter essay about the notorious French libertine and pornographer the Marquis de Sade, having spent the previous few weeks with those same adults considering Primo Levi's account of conditions in Auschwitz and Hannah Arendt's concept of the 'banality of evil'. And the expectation appeared to be that I would rush out in the middle of a busy semester to fulfil this suddenly mandatory requirement, even though I was, like a good proportion of the teaching staff at universities these days, not a permanent employee, but a casual with no leave entitlements or job security, who was being paid an hourly rate that did not include preparation or consultation time, and whose services would be dispensed with the moment the final essay was marked at the semester's end.

Christ on a bike, I thought. What will they want next? A heavy vehicle licence? A responsible service of alcohol certificate? An Estonian tourist visa? So I did what a reasonable person would do when faced with such a reasonable demand: I placed it in the far queue and busied myself with more pressing matters. I would deal with that particular edict, I told myself, if and when someone decided to follow it up – guessing (correctly, as it turned out) that no one was likely to be doing so any time soon.

That same semester, I was asked, again at short notice, to teach another course at a different university. Such is the nature of casual employment in the tertiary sector. This university did not require employees to submit to irrelevant police checks. In order to establish that I was a virtuous person, I was merely required to complete an online training module about ethical behaviour. This consisted of a series of hypothetical scenarios, which I was to grade on a scale from one to five. Some of these scenarios were straightforward (sleeping with students: totally not ethical – I got that one right); others occupied more of a 'grey area', as the online module helpfully explained when I assigned a three to a particularly dicey ethical conundrum that should have been scored a two.

Anyway, after I failed, I was given the option to complete the module again. I confess that I had not been taking the exercise all that seriously up to that point, as you were allowed multiple attempts to get it right. My initial run through had merely been to gain a sense of what I was being asked to do. And it was impossible to fail, really, if you put your mind to it, because the university supplied a glossy brochure that explained the finer points of each ethically challenging situation and set out clear behavioural expectations. All you had to do was scan the PDF and find the answer they wanted. The possibility that this might allow an unethical person to slip through their vetting process had apparently not occurred to them.

But I decided not to persist, again guessing correctly that the labyrinthine administrative superstructure of the modern corporatised university was such that there was unlikely to be anyone rushing to reprimand me for neglecting this bureaucratic obligation. What bugged me about it was not just the pointless box-ticking and the minor irritation of being told how to behave, even though I had relevant qualifications and experience, and despite the fact that I was (I liked to think) an adequately socialised human being – no, what really irked me was the apparent correlation between the version of 'ethical' behaviour this slick training module was seeking to impose and the imperative not to act in any way that might besmirch the good name of the university. It was all about protecting the brand. The assumption seemed to be that behaving ethically and maintaining high academic standards were important, not because we have personal and professional obligations towards other people, or because the very purpose of the university was to nurture the life of the mind and encourage scholarly endeavours as noble ends in themselves, but because these things were excellent for public relations and likely to generate high levels of customer satisfaction.

Now, I realise this is all pretty trivial. Like the demand that someone who does not work with children undergo a 'working with children' check, the online module was a mere formality, little more than a symbolic gesture, the kind of tick-and-flick exercise that bureaucracies like to impose every once in a while to remind everyone just who is working for whom. It probably warranted no greater show of resistance than the theatrical eye-roll performed by the young academic who told me about this particular requirement.

Unfortunately, however, I have a background in literary studies. As a result, I tend to treat questions of language and symbolism as if they are important. It is literally the only thing I am qualified to do. I have been trained to regard even small symbolic gestures as significant precisely because they encapsulate larger structures of meaning. This made it hard to overlook the arrogation of virtue. The university was, in essence, rigging up its probity by demanding I prove my own. It was seeking to indemnify itself. Yet it seemed to me that the convenient conflation of virtue and self-interest in this instance, when set against the actual conduct of the university, could be readily interpreted as evidence of systemic hypocrisy.

Here was an educational institution making a show of its commitment to the highest standards of professional behaviour and the welfare of its students, at the same time as it was funnelling as many students as possible through outrageously overcrowded and understaffed courses, and outsourcing much of the substance of the education they were there to receive to sessional teachers, like me, who were not being provided with the kinds of working conditions that might allow them to do their jobs to the best of their ability, or being remunerated at levels that even began to approach adequacy. Here, in short, was an institution demanding a ritual show of obeisance without burdening itself with any reciprocal sense of obligation, an institution that clearly had no qualms about treating casual employees and students alike as exploitable and disposable.

Did I mention that the 'ethics' of this particular university do not preclude hiring someone for two hours a week, then expecting that person to take sole responsibility for a cohort of almost eighty students?

—

I raise all of this for a number of reasons. The first is that, if we are going to talk about scholarship, it is necessary to get the admin out of the way. The second is to declare that I cannot claim to be a scholar in any professional sense, as no university has ever troubled itself to employ me in an ongoing capacity. Most of my work over the past twenty years has taken the contingent form of public criticism, which I have pursued in the faint hope that it might be possible to carve out a little space to read and think and write about literature beyond the walls of the academy. Anything I have to say on the subject of scholarship thus comes from a marginal and, as it were, undomesticated perspective.

And from this vantage point things would appear to be less than optimal. It seems to me that the starting point for any discussion of the meaning and value of scholarship – and I am assuming we are talking predominantly about scholarship within the discipline of literary studies, though I take this to be a reflection of the situation with regard to the humanities more broadly – must be how scholars themselves are treated by the institutions that notionally exist to foster such scholarship. This would suggest that we live in a society that is devaluing scholarship in a quite literal sense. In May 2019, *The Age* reported that around two-thirds of the academic staff at Victorian universities had no secure or ongoing employment. The ratio at the state's two wealthiest and most prestigious universities, Melbourne and Monash – universities that in 2018 boasted a combined revenue of more than $3.5 billion – was over seventy per cent.

Those figures, which reflect national and international trends towards the casualisation of academic labour, are frankly disgusting. The official line that sessional teachers are paid for all the hours they work is plainly a lie. Systemic exploitation on such a scale cannot be regarded as a minor or incidental feature of the contemporary university. As one frustrated casual academic was moved to observe recently, we have to confront the fact that ripping off sessional teachers while grinding them into the dirt is now part of the business model. The academic quislings whose response to this development is to ponder its potential 'benefits', while blandly predicting that rates of casualisation will only increase, or who greet the prospect of a generation of emerging scholars being forced into an unconscionable state of precarity with the inane observation that 'we will all need to be custodians of our own Brand Me', should be ashamed of themselves. I do, however, salute whoever wrote the headline for the first of the articles I am alluding to, which perfectly captures the Helleresque absurdity of this academic version of Stockholm Syndrome: 'Casual academics aren't going anywhere, so what can universities do to ensure learning isn't affected?'

It is not just the proposition that educational standards can somehow be separated from the disgraceful material conditions under which casual academics are expected to work that makes you want to claw your own eyes out. What is truly dispiriting is the sense of resignation, the assumption that the obvious answer to the question is unthinkable. Apparently, all those overworked and underpaid casuals should stop hitting themselves. The passive acceptance of the idea that (to quote Margaret Thatcher) 'there is no alternative' represents a clear victory for the prevailing corporate ideology, which recognises no principle beyond its expansionist logic of ever-increasing turnover and maximised revenue. The unambiguous implication of such thinking is that academics exist to support the system, rather than the other way round. So much for the idea of a self-governing community of scholars.

Again, I stress that I am viewing this from an external perspective, and I am well aware that academics have been complaining about managerialism and lamenting the fate of the humanities from time immemorial. But I can't recall a time when the discipline of literary studies, in particular, has seemed as besieged and vulnerable as its does at present. Literature departments are shadows of their former selves. The attrition rate among young literary scholars in the United States has been described as an 'extinction event' and has even spawned its own sub-genre of essay known as 'quit-lit', in which former academics recount their tales of being burnt out and walking away in disgust.

The fact that for several decades the study of literature has been the focus of fierce ideological dispute has also taken its toll. We have reached the point where prominent right-wing voices in Britain and the United States are openly canvassing the possibility of defunding or abolishing the humanities altogether. Relentless culture warring has hollowed out the notion that studying literature is an intellectually valid occupation in itself. To the extent that it retains a degree of cultural significance, it has become a symbolic chattel to be squabbled over. Public discussions about its potential value as art and its inherent complexities have been subsumed by demarcation disputes and simple-minded political arguments, in which the *substance* of specific works of literature is essentially moot. There could hardly be a more brazen insult to the innumerable scholars who have devoted themselves to the study of literature than the spectacle of a well-funded coterie of ideological cranks, self-appointed defenders of 'Western Civilisation', who plainly couldn't give a toss about anything Milton or Flaubert might have had to say, walking into a Vice-Chancellor's office with a cheque for $50 million and walking out with their very own custom-designed vanity degree.

—

The traditional defence of the humanities has its intellectual roots in late eighteenth-century romanticism, from which emerged the notion of 'aesthetic education': the idea that exposure to great art and literature will have a civilising or refining effect, that it will open a path to the holistic process of personal growth and self-realisation encapsulated by the German concept *Bildung*. This idea has, for a host of reasons, come to be viewed with justified scepticism. The late George Steiner once pointed out – conclusively, one would think – that there were officers at Auschwitz who liked to relax after a hard day's genocide with a volume of Goethe's poetry and a Beethoven record playing on the gramophone (and fair play to whoever noted that one need not reach for such an extreme example, since the proposition that literature has a civilising effect is disproved by a quick glance at any university English department).

But in the stubborn notion, to which I retain a sometimes uneasy allegiance, that serious literature has things to teach us, that it represents something more substantial and important than a mere idle diversion, resides a basic ambiguity that defines the humanities – namely, that it has a foundational commitment to an ideal of intellectual inquiry that is autotelic. The value of its scholarship cannot ultimately be quantified, precisely because it recognises that man does not live by bread alone. The humanities are premised on the idea that to be 'human' means having a natural interest in the true, the beautiful and the good.

That such sentiments, with their suspicious whiff of the ineffable, have come to seem platitudinous is an indication of how naturalised they once were, and how fundamental they once were to the very conception of the university. Even a confirmed utilitarian like John Stuart Mill could acknowledge, as something of a commonplace, the intrinsic value of an open-ended, anti-instrumentalist view of education. The university, he observed, 'is not a place of professional education. Universities are not intended to teach the knowledge required to fit men for some special mode of gaining their livelihood. Their object is not to make skilful lawyers, or physicians, or engineers, but capable and cultivated human beings.'

The problem we now face – and by 'we' I mean those of us who still believe that literature constitutes a substantive body of cultural knowledge worth preserving and studying – is not simply the traditional scepticism about the value of an education in the humanities, but a pervasive set of cultural assumptions that have made it difficult to speak of literature *as* a substantive body of knowledge.

In his recent book *Nervous States*, the British sociologist William Davies argues that the 'post-truth' society we now inhabit, with its overt scorn for the very notion of expertise, is the logical outcome of the ideas of Friedrich Hayek, who is universally recognised as the intellectual godfather of the neoliberalism that has been restructuring our lives for the better part of four decades. Hayek wrote in opposition to any and all forms of socialistic thought, basing his philosophy on the contrary notion of a radically atomised version of *Homo economicus*. In doing so, he not only repudiated communism and even the mildest forms of democratic socialism, but essential components of traditional liberalism as well. One can take as an indication of just how comprehensively Hayek has eclipsed his nearest ideological rivals the fact that Davies' wide-ranging intellectual history, which reaches back to the seventeenth century in its attempt to identify the philosophical foundations of our current predicament, charts the rise of so-called 'neoliberalism' without feeling the need to refer to the likes of Locke, Mill and Rawls even in passing.

The assumed obsolescence of these canonical liberal philosophers underscores the essential point, since it is precisely what is 'liberal' about them that neoliberalism vanquishes. Mill's famous defence of free speech proposed that the truth can only emerge from a process of unfettered debate. In the present climate, that might seem optimistic, but Mill at least assumes that there is such a thing as truth and that it might be discoverable. At the heart of Rawls' thought is the concept of justice: the difficult problem of how to balance the liberal commitment to the rights of the individual against the need for social cohesion and fairness. Mill and Rawls, in other words, predicate their individualism on a negotiated relationship with a social realm and with metaphysical concepts that are assumed to be held in common – which is to say, there is a humanistic core to their thinking, an assumption that while we might never agree what constitutes truth and justice, we can at least agree that truth and justice are the subjects of dispute, and that they are ends worth pursuing.

This is, more or less, the basic paradigm of scholarship. As Davies points out, the starchy formalities of scholarly discourse arose in order to avoid personalising the business of intellectual disputation: you can attack someone's ideas as vigorously as you like, but you must respect your colleagues. This convention, imperfectly practised though it often is, recognises that scholarship entails a process of negotiation between individual expertise and an accepted body of knowledge; it is a way of negotiating the inevitable friction between one's own experiences and convictions and those of other people, from which emerges the possibility of an expanded and enriched understanding. It assumes that genuine knowledge is grounded in evidence and reason, that to be credited as such it must be able to withstand scrutiny, demonstrate that it is based on something more substantial than a personal opinion. Thus individual scholars, however singular their views, both draw upon and contribute to a collective endeavour.

The defining characteristic of neoliberalism – and, Davies suggests, its most diabolical innovation – is that it does not even *try* to negotiate these kinds of tensions. It simply dismisses them. It is a philosophy that has more in common with Sade than Rawls. It recognises no principle beyond individual desires, accepts the validity of no collective measure of those desires beyond the hard data of the marketplace. This means, in effect, that it makes no distinction between a baseless conviction and an expert opinion. As Davies observes, its attitude to truth can be summed up in a remark attributed to Napoleon: 'It is not what is true that counts, but what people think is true.' It is a view of the world that is not merely philistine; it has been conceived in such a way that it is *incapable* of registering the value of any kind of meaningful abstract concept that speaks to our inner being or to our collective existence – not only truth and justice, but beauty, morality, society, and of course the proposition that an education in the humanities might have a value that has no valid metric, that its greatest value may well be that it refuses to submit to narrow instrumentalist thinking.

On a purely institutional level, this inevitably ends up validating the tyranny of the majority that Mill cautioned against, bending the scholarly function of the university to meet the demands of the marketplace. The calculus is simple. Popular courses thrive; unpopular courses die. Research that attracts external funding is important; research that does not is unimportant. Utility is all. I am grateful to the federal education minister Dan Tehan for stepping forward, at the very moment I was sitting down to write this paper, to demonstrate the point. In the course of announcing that the funding goalpoasts for universities were to be moved once again, he declared that literary scholarship was otiose. Soon it will disappear once and for all; it will wither and die, and good riddance to all that useless cultural knowledge. I am paraphrasing, of course. What he actually said was that our universities must be 'producing job-ready graduates with the right skills for the modern economy', which amounts to much the same thing.

To this end, Tehan announced that funding was to be linked to a new set of metrics that would not only quantify internal practices, but take account of graduate employment outcomes. Now, I realise that the world is facing far greater problems than arcane funding arrangements for beleaguered humanities departments, and we are all numbed to this kind of thing, but I am quietly astonished that this announcement didn't seem to generate much of a ripple. If humanities departments are, on top of everything else, going to be held responsible for what happens to students *after* they graduate, then we may as well admit it's all over – though it must be conceded that the system will be approaching something close to perfection when it becomes possible to accumulate an enormous student debt completing a university degree in literary studies, taught almost exclusively by academics without secure jobs, only to become an exploited casual who is paid for a fraction of the hours you work, at which point the cash-strapped department that lacked the resources to employ you properly in the first place will face additional funding cuts because your quantifiable 'graduate outcome' indicates that you didn't earn enough money.

The simple point I am trying to make is that if you set out to justify literary scholarship in utilitarian terms, you have lost the argument before you start. To my mind, scholarship is a word with overwhelmingly positive connotations. I regard it as distinct from the related concepts of research and theorisation, which are the necessary activities one undertakes in order to arrive at some kind of genuine understanding. Scholarship represents the knowledge itself. It is the ideal. It evokes the positive principles of intellectual rigour and disinterestedness, in the true meaning of that word. It speaks of a love of knowledge for its own sake, a desire to understand things in all their complexity. It rejects impulsive or emotive interpretations, preferring the kind of grounded and measured view that can only be arrived at through a consideration of all the available facts. It is not divorced from political concerns, but it is fundamentally non-ideological and anti-instrumentalist in its orientation. Its allegiance is always to that which is true, that which is verifiable. The true scholar respects the evidence, respects precedent and expertise, and argues in good faith, even when taking a dissenting line. Scholarship is thus communal; it opens up the shared realms of culture and knowledge, demands a consideration of abstract values and concerns larger than our own.

By this definition, scholarship is implacably opposed, in every important respect, to the political and institutional culture we now face. This is precisely why the ideal is worth upholding, why it urgently needs to be defended, but also why defending it can seem like such a thankless task. I am not in a position to offer any concrete solutions to this dilemma, but I will make a general observation. Over the past four decades or so, much of the theoretical work within the humanities has flattered itself with the idea that it is intrinsically radical. Literary scholars have been busy dismantling canons, subverting dominant paradigms, practising the hermeneutics of suspicion, insisting on the radical indeterminacy of language, using words like 'essentialist' and 'normative' as insults, and so forth. I am far from the first person to note that there is a certain historical irony in the fact that humanities scholars have been busy reading their Foucault while the universities have been morphing into panopticons, or that the kinds of sociological approaches and abstruse philosophising that have characterised these theoretical developments could be interpreted as convenient means of adapting to institutional demands. And my intention here is not to dismiss or even denigrate the intellectual substance of these phenomena, which are far too complex and diffuse to admit any easy judgement. I would merely observe that one of the consequences of all this theorising for literary studies has been an evident loss of faith in itself, an inability and perhaps even a squeamishness about articulating a positive argument in its own defence.

There has been something of a move away from this tendency of late. As Rita Felski has observed, the habit of treating literary works as symptomatic, rather than substantive in themselves, leaves unanswered the question of why one might choose to read them in the first place. This sentiment has been echoed by Toril Moi, who argues in her latest book *Revolution of the Ordinary* that the anti-essentialist thinking that has come to predominate within the humanities remains 'trapped in negation' – which is to say, it defines itself in the act of rejection, leaving itself unable to articulate any valid principle of its own. Moi's specific ambition in *Revolution of the Ordinary* is to propose a version of Wittgenstein's ordinary language philosophy as an alternative to what she sees as the dead end of post-Saussurean thought. But in the process she makes a straightforward point. 'Much of the humanities deals in particulars,' she writes. 'The critic's love for the particular case – the specific poem, novel, or film, the specific artist, painting, composition – fuels her work.' This is a truth that literary scholars are apt to downplay, if not conceal. If the challenge before us is to find a way to argue for the value of literary studies that resonates beyond a shrinking community of beleaguered scholars, then I am inclined to agree with Moi that the way forward lies with dropping certain pretenses to theoretical sophistication, speaking of the substance of literature in meaningful ways that emphasise its specificity and its relevance, developing a plain-spoken poetics that is grounded in appreciation and attentiveness. I don't necessarily think this will fix anything, but it couldn't hurt.

Loss Statement

Eda Gunaydin

I'm letting our succulents die. I was the only one keeping them alive. So I've forced myself to stop. I read in a book that a vital stage of healing for those who have sustained trauma is *letting go of the caretaker roles they find oppressive*. I have deleted from my calendar the reminder notification that says 'water plant'. When I see the pots I force myself to look away, and resist the compulsion to run to their aid.

In 2018, around about this time, I was in Mudgee for the annual Readers' Festival. Before the lockdown came into effect in June of 2021, my friends and I were planning to go back again this year. Now cancelled, its future, like that of other regional writing festivals, seems uncertain. I remember, three years ago, on Market Street, seeing a small jade plant in a public flowerbed that had toppled. Picking it up and righting it, I pushed it back firmly into the soil, and said out loud, to myself, 'Oh no, this poor succulent has fallen down.' Some patrons at a nearby café, in earshot of me, laughed, finding what I had said and done, I guess, endearing or whimsical. I think of that person now, as I apply myself to desiccating these fuckers in my yard slowly to death.

—

I clean under the bed. I clean the whole house, compulsively, day and night, and it develops a kind of spinstery smell: cigarettes and bleach. I am surprised in particular by the way that the bedroom floor had seemed spotless, until I peeked under the furniture. The bits of the house you can't see are filthy; the house only seemed clean. Boring metaphor. I fill a garbage bag with clumps of hair and dust, used tissues, lost slippers, forsaken hair ties, my favourite pens. I am not writing.

—

A colleague and I meet on Zoom every Friday, keeping each other up till past midnight, the conversation sometimes devolving into incoherent gurgling as we use each other's companionship to fall asleep. We discuss the issue of whether I should or should not let go of a friend of three years who has, I keep insisting, been unable to be there for me during my recent dark night of the soul, my flowery way of talking about an unexpected break-up with my partner of eight years during a lockdown that has me now living alone.

My colleague insists that one should never burn a bridge. *Keep watering the plant, just in case. Remember, it's a pandemic. We're all burnt out right now. He'll come back soon.*

I acknowledge that he is right, but, and yet. *I'm sorry,* I find myself insisting. *I appreciate your advice. But I can't. I'm sorry, I can't.* I continue, *I just – I never get to be the shitty one, you know? I never get to be the dud, the flop, the crazy one. When do I get to suck?*

Hold on! he interrupts. *Hold on!*

I shout back, *no, you hold on!*

But he carries on, speaking over me: *Hold on! Who are these people who 'get to be crazy'?*

I think of a tweet: ninety-five per cent of Twitter is people making up a person and then getting mad at them. We both collapse into giggles.

—

During this period I have been incapable of doing anything: positively haemorrhaging cash, deadlines (which used to structure my day-to-day existence), and career goals (which used to propel me) feel distant and insubstantial. I develop the habit of weakly remarking about some missed deadline or another, 'What are they gonna do, come to my house?'

I have to push back my PhD thesis submission deadline by six months. I submit two thirds of my book manuscript to my publisher, and then shit the bed on completing the final three essays: for a few months, I could not even tell you what their titles were meant to be, or who is the Me who was meant to be narrating them. The only thing that penetrates my brain fog is reading books on psychology – which is where I got the phrase *dark night of the soul* – and taking copious voice memos and Google Keep notes, in which I detail my dreams, and variously reflect on feelings that come up around my divorce. In one, I comment that I am so grateful I have such an active subconscious, which processes things for me on my behalf. For example: in one dream, my house is about to explode, and I know it is, and my former partner knows it is too. An hour before the scheduled eruption, I get up out of bed, sneak away from my partner. I crack a window, and I practise escaping, and then I slip back into bed and lie in wait. My partner decides not to do any preparation, and in the dream he dies and I become a widow. I wake up, both grateful that I practise escaping and afraid that from now on I will always practise escaping.

In another memo, I comment that my brain is a souped-up trauma-processing machine. My subconscious works even while I am not working. I sleep and it cleans shop.

On Twitter, the Elizabeth Jolley bot posts: 'Leaves fall all the time and new leaves come, stained bark.' When I go to copy it out into a Note, I accidentally write, 'Leaves fall all the time and feel like a punishment.' Did I write that?

—

One attempt my colleagues and I make to stay tethered to one another is through a reading group. Each of us gets to take a turn to pick the book, which we meet weekly in order, sometimes, to excoriate. Occasionally we pause to acknowledge that each of us will someday go on to publish a book, and that we hope our critics will be kind. But that future is yet to come, and so in the meantime we run our mouths. Occasionally, we ironically repeat the tweet, 'Congrats to anyone who has ever written a book,' a shorthand means of acknowledging that it is in fact a difficult feat. *Writing a book is worthy of respect,* says my colleague, about one particular text that he hates. Setting up for an even more brutal takedown by first feigning graciousness. *But the real issue here is that this does not even meet the definition of a book.* We hoot and holler like schoolkids over the quality of this roast.

When it rolls around to my turn, I pick Sophie Lewis' *Full Surrogacy Now,* a work that advocates, among other things, for the abolition of the family. It makes sense for me in a way it doesn't make sense for my peers. During one meeting, I find myself insisting, only half-jokingly, that *we are all already each other's mothers! We are! And therefore the family is an unnatural construct!* But only someone motherless would believe that.

I haven't seen my mother in months. Normally, she occupies a significant portion of my mental real estate. She looms large, especially in my work, but this period – of physical distance, and of *letting go of the caretaker roles I find oppressive* – has allowed her to recede. I am worried that soon I won't care enough anymore about the impact her life experiences have had on mine, and that therefore I will no longer be able to reliably tap the vein that has so far animated my work. I am worried I can't work, that I will never feel well – or even ill – enough to work again.

In *Full Surrogacy Now*, Lewis quotes a line from Maggie Nelson's *The Argonauts*, which, anyway, is Maggie Nelson quoting something she was told many times in the lead-up to giving birth to her and her partner's child Iggy.

You don't do labour – labour does you.

Congrats to anyone who is writing their book.

—

Yet another note, under the heading COMFORT, reads, 'Grief involves the pain of losing something that we had. But we didn't always have it; as with dying and returning to non-existence, all that we're doing is going back to a prior state, before we had what we had.'

None of this writing is the right writing, but this writing rights me.

—

I get used to telling my friends the CliffsNotes version of the break-up story. I do it about eight times before I stop being able to be bothered – before I hang up my gloves, stop touring the material. I have synthesised a tight, condensed, although admittedly forty-minute – and therefore neither tight nor condensed – version. Each time I tell it, I feel myself perfecting the content, hitting different beats, setting up a few Chekhov's guns: remember this name, it becomes important later; remember this conversation. 'Play stupid games, win stupid prizes,' is one of the lines I repeat, as it gets me a sure laugh every time.

My friend Tim comes by and drops me off a copy of Rachel Cusk's *Aftermath. For research,* he says.

True, I say, laughing. *Maybe some day this'll be an essay. I actually already have the title picked out.* But I'm not writing it.

When I tell my publisher I might be late on delivering the last essay of the book, the real book, the one I have under deadline, she is understanding and commiserative.

'That sounds so hard,' she says.

'Eh, it's alright,' I say. Don't know why I harbour the impulse to slap away words of comfort. 'And anyway, it's all material, right?' We both laugh weakly.

—

I obsess over a print I bought my former partner – due to Covid lockdowns, I purchase it before the break-up, and by the time he and I are wrapped it hasn't even shipped from Melbourne. I can't quite parse that a tracking number can outlive a relationship, or that we must satisfy this injunction that the universe has placed on us that we play out interpersonal crises in the background of the collapse of the global political economy. We are like pianolas with the notes pre-loaded.

I forget about the print I have ordered until one night I wake at 4 a.m. in a lurch, unable to think about anything else. I email the artist. The print was a gift in recognition of an important career milestone. When it does arrive, I contemplate writing something deranged down the side of the mailing tube, like, 'Congratulations!

I thought that this was something we achieved together. I thought this was for both of us. I thought this was a shared investment.' But I don't; I hand it over, in the form of the unladen gift it was once intended to be. I am not writing on the tube.

—

I don't write. I take walks. Some days I walk for up to four hours, either alone or cycling through a range of different companions that I am lucky enough to have living within five kilometres of me.

On Zoom, when I speak to my colleague, he often insists that he viscerally loves his home city, yearns for it like nothing else. I used to often remind him that he was responding to a question I hadn't asked: who *do you love?* I would say, Who, *not where. You have to name a person.*

But I don't care about this question anymore. It is easy to love Rozelle Bay. Every morning, I drive, possessed, to smell the bay's air, to look over the smattering of moored boats, to watch the sun glint and reflect off the water. Maybe this is an asymmetric, and therefore degraded, form of love – I cannot act on this place but it can act on me.

Tim and I walk Rozelle Bay every week, and we discuss my break-up, the beats of which sometimes reflect events that have occurred in his own life. One night, he ponders aloud, 'Isn't it crazy that we're all going through the same kinds of feelings, the same big life changes, just with endless permutations in terms of tweaks in minor details, like the themes are the same but the plot is different?'

'I wouldn't know,' I say, attempting a joke. 'I don't write anymore.'

—

My nails are growing back out. For years this has been the key way for me to tell how my subconscious is doing. At the most stressful junctures of my life, I have stubs, red fingertips, peppered with dried blood. I have to use these clues because I don't have the insight that I pretend to – I often am only guessing at myself. My friend Marie, who joins my singles bubble – oh, how my former partner and I had pitied people who lived alone during the lockdowns, until – points out that I didn't practise escaping, really. What happened did blindside me. Maybe it was convenient for me to believe that I had known the whole time. *Maybe some part of you knew,* she says. *But most of you didn't.* We are drinking beer on my couch, at the end of a long week for her, and the end of yet another one of my 'weeks off', so called because I have been helpless to accomplish anything. I am not writing, I have not been writing, I am not working, I have not been working. But this week I might start again.

Pandemic Soundtrack

Sunil Badami

As a writer, I'm always thinking two or three sentences ahead, two or three pages ahead, two or three chapters ahead, and back again, the process of writing much like thought itself, jumping from one place to another, like a chattering monkey leaping from branch to branch: moments and memories and ideas sparking and flashing and rustling like an erratic breeze through the leaves.

And yet, there are times when I'm so immersed in what I'm writing or reading that I forget the time, my aching back, my numb leg, the press and thrum of my worries and neuroses, wondering if what I'm writing is any good, how I'll pay the bills, what the point of calling out into an increasingly noisy void of social media and fake news and the chyron streaming across the screen screaming at me how many cases, how many job losses, how many deaths, how much is happening and how little I know, and how much less I can do.

If this pandemic has revealed anything – apart from the fragility of capitalism, and the necessity of touch, and the dangerous infectiousness of fear and ignorance – it's the fallacy of certainty: what we thought would be now might never be; what we thought could happen tomorrow probably won't.

As the child of Indian immigrants, my future was as clearly predestined as the horoscope the purohit charted at my birth. I'd study hard, become a doctor, make my mother proud. Medicine is what brought my parents here, under the long shadow of the White Australia Policy.

It gave them the semblance of status that their cheap clothes and pungent food and sing-song accents and gaucheness with cutlery belied, all of which constantly reminded them, and me, in Blacktown's hot bitumen playgrounds, that we would never be quite Australian enough, no matter how hard we tried to disavow our noisy, unintelligible Indianness.

I hated always being reminded of where I 'really' came from: it was never Blacktown, or Australia, though I was born here, and despite the timorous shoots of multiculturalism supposedly celebrating our difference, my parents never taught me their languages. By the time my father had left my mother, the only Indian words I could ever speak were ones I'd heard them shout at each other in anger (the first time I tried to speak my father's language, to try and impress on his cold, old mother that I was, ironically, Indian enough, she was so shocked at the words I used, she slapped me).

I hated it when my mother made us sing monotonal, monotonous, unpronounceable Sanskrit bhajjans and slokas before school, in that long dead language, which meant nothing to me – not compared to the hymns we sang at school, where the invisible *Eternal Father, strong to save, whose arm hath bounded the restless wave and midst the mighty ocean deep its own appointed limits keep* meant more to me in English, the language people mocked my mother's inability to speak 'properly', than the songs and colourful idols she held close, fluttering as tremblingly as the lamp in the little cupboard she kept the brass idols her own mother had given her, burnished by her fervent prayers and fading hope.

I remember now with shame dreaming of how and when I could escape her tight embrace, even though I and my brother were now her only family in the world, or at least the world she'd made out of the ashes of her marriage, so far from everyone and everything she loved.

When I read *On the Road* by Jack Kerouac, and met dharma bum Sal Paradise hitting that wide open road, full of the crazy rhythms of bebop and poetry and thrumming with adventure, writing, writing, writing – and living, living, living – without thought or consequence, I knew I'd never be a doctor, and all I wanted was something more, anything else, anything but the deadening sound of those ancient mantras washing over me like the echoing whispers of countless generations and expectations, reminding me over and over how un-Australian we were.

When I first listened to bebop, it was like when I started listening to thrash metal, or had my first beer, or smoked my first cigarette: I couldn't understand how anyone could like it. But as Kierkegaard famously observed, we pursue that which retreats from us, whether it's an acquired taste, or unrequited love, or Australianness.

And as I persisted, and heard more (and drank, and smoked, and desired more), the more I heard exactly what Miles Davis meant when he said it wasn't the notes he played, but the ones he didn't, and the more I understood what August Strindberg meant when he observed that we often use words to hide the meaning conveyed by the silence between them.

Silence, as you may have surmised from this prolix reflection so far, is not easy for me. Although I can spend most of the day not speaking to another person, even my wife and children as we're locked down in the house together, my head is full of voices: my characters, interview subjects, my father's, my mother's. But I cannot listen to music with lyrics: I've ended up transcribing it as I'm writing, in that liminal place between consciousness and mindfulness, between awareness and aliveness, when more than forgetting the trivialities I mentioned before, I forget myself and lose myself in my work.

And yet, where I could find a kind of purchase on the erratic, improvised rhythms and atonalities of hard bop (or the relentless raucousness of thrash metal), Indian classic music, especially the South Indian Carnatic music my mother loved, was as unintelligible as her own mother tongue: it was just noise, going nowhere, saying nothing to me.

I struggled to follow it, just I failed to understand the distinctions between Vedanta and Advaita – and whether my soul was just an indistinguishable drop in the ocean or the crest of a wave, only superficially different, but ultimately the same as the water it was a part of.

Much less the idea of Atman: utter, utterless, unimaginable unconsciousness! For someone always so self-conscious of my Westieness, my Indianness, myself, it was unbelievable.

And in my cruel, callow youth, I thought it ridiculous that my mother would continue to light the lamp to her two favourite gods, elephant-headed Ganapati and flute-playing Krishna, her voice quiet and shy as she sang those old slokas alone, afraid of my disdain, her idolatry at odds with those impenetrable philosophical problems.

One of my favourite musicians was always John Coltrane. There was something about him that was both poetic and rock'n'roll: the quiet thoughtfulness of his music, his tragic early death. And my favourite Coltrane album was 1965's *A Love Supreme*, one of the greatest jazz albums ever, an album that soars and swoops from the opening notes, like a swan about to take flight across shimmering water.

Music, especially jazz, is like a flowering vine, the notes branching out, like a great banyan tree into other directions, even seeming to be other trees, although like the great Tree of Knowledge in Adyar in Chennai, near my mother's family, they are but the same.

Given the great blooming of ground-breaking talent in the 1950s and 1960s – Coltrane, Miles Davis, Charlie Byrd, Dizzy Gillespie, Thelonius Monk, many of whom Coltrane had played with – it was natural to explore them all, each leading to the other, each of them infusing each other's music.

Of course, had I been more perceptive, I'd have realised that the complicated rhythms and unpredictable syncopations in bebop most resembled the Carnatic classical music my mother loved, the underlying melody a trellis allowing the music to discover its own path, with no idea where or how it would go or end up.

Much like living in a pandemic.

And then I discovered Coltrane's widow, Alice. I remember that now long-closed record shop in Bondi where I first saw the cover. It was pouring with rain, the mist blurring the raging waves out to sea. She was sitting in a paisley kaftan, looking somewhere else, a distant look on her face, and I saw my own face, sitting in temples and ashrams with my mother after our father left, my legs aching and bored, wishing I was somewhere else, doing anything else, mouthing words I couldn't speak as we chanted bhajjans for what seemed like hours.

What struck me most was the title: *Journey in Satchidananda*. Not Satchidananda, the famous swami from Chettypalayam, not far from where my mother's family now lived, after they'd lost everything to Naxalite Maoists? From the same, dry, dusty, forgotten, faraway corner of South India, much like Blacktown: a place people passed through, not where they went? Even he had left for America years ago.

Now, of course, yoga and meditation and vegetarianism are all fashionable – and profitable. But then, when I first held that record, I was both astonished and ashamed. Why would this American musician be interested in something so Indian? And why couldn't I be?

From the first notes, a swirl of harp that sounded much like a sitar, I was entranced. It was as if, translated by jazz, I suddenly heard the magic I hadn't seen. I listened to the album over and over and over and whenever I felt stressed or alone or sad, I'd listen to it and it wouldn't just wash over me but course through me, each track leading on from the other just as each note did. And although in parts it's exultant, there's a deep, reflective sadness pervading the music, of sorrow and loss and acceptance.

Alice Coltrane had had a multitude of lives before that journey into Satchidananda: classical musician, gospel accompanist, big band leader, jazz prodigy, her knowledge and experience of all these different forms informing and interacting with each other, especially in the way she played classical harp.

Wife, mother, bandleader...and then, in the 1970s, after unbearable grief following her husband's death (and around the same time as my father left my mother) she became a swamini, or spiritual leader, establishing her own ashram and devoting herself to prayer and meditation, changing her name to Turiyasangitananda, turning her back on commercial recording and only singing for her disciples.

I've listened to a lot of her music in the past eighteen

months. There are moments when I am just as transported and unselfconscious as I am when I'm writing, really writing, and I lose myself in the music, as I sometimes do in the writing.

It's been a solace, especially now, when I cannot see my mother, who is safe but alone in her nursing home due to lockdown. I am unable to touch her or console her as each lonely, indistinguishable day passes into another, her past life as a doctor now distant, as she increasingly is, lost in her memories, or at least those she can remember.

Earlier this year, as Sydney's lockdown extended into an uncertain duration, and our future seemed increasingly unpredictable, a new album was released, produced by Turiya's son Ravi, from old cassettes she recorded only for devotees at the ashram called *Kirtan: Turiya Sings*.

Although I was familiar with her music, I'd never heard her voice, and now, it is a revelation. She sounds at once distant and intimate, her voice faraway and so close – like so many of us right now in lockdown. Her voice, especially on the elegiac *Krishna Krishna*, sounds as if it is floating above water – just as the first sound, OM, did before time began, or the Word of God did over those restless seas. You cannot expect a chorus or a refrain: you can only immerse yourself in the music and let it happen, without expectation, and let it carry you to places you could never have imagined.

It's haunting to hear Turiya's long-dead voice so alive, and make you feel so alive, even as you cannot understand the ancient words she intones in that long-dead language, Sanskrit.

And yet, you do. Not because you can comprehend what they say, but because you feel what they mean. *Jai Ramachandra,*

Govinda Hari, Pranadhana...all the words my mother taught me to say, all flooding back to me, remembering lives long lost, including my own, in a country where they always did things differently: the past, which, given the increasing uncertainty of the future, seems realer than ever before.

Like good writing, great music connects us to each other, and enables us to imagine beyond ourselves, without thinking of the repercussions, only experiencing the moment. It acknowledges what we've suffered alone, and in accepting this, exhorts and inspires us to come together, going beyond words.

In an eloquent and perceptive review of the album and Turiya's work and significance, critic Jenn Pelly said that '[her] compositions make you feel connected to yourself and the world with preternatural clarity. They make you believe things you otherwise wouldn't; they may even facilitate the process of temporarily suspending fear.'

More than this, they make me not only feel connected to myself (whoever that is) and the generations of ancestors before me who sang such songs in the same words, but to my mother, and everything she left behind to bring us here, and even as my own children look at me with similar disdain when I try to teach them a little of our heritage, I somehow feel I finally understand. Although we're still apart, we're a little bit closer.

On Being a Precedent

Fiona Wright

It was in January last year, in 2020, that Scott Morrison first used the phrase *new normal.* In that particular instance he was referring to the deployment of Defence personnel and resources in response to the devastating bushfires that were raging across the country at the time (and no, he didn't mention climate change as the larger, more pressing *new normal* facing our whole world). It's a strange and infuriating usage, even taken without the context of everything that happened next, for the way it insists that we accept as normal a way of dealing with a consequence, without also accepting its cause or any steps that we might take to mitigate it. But it's a usage that was rapidly forgotten – by late March, with the pandemic in full swing, it seemed mandatory to include the words *new normal* in any headline, just as it was to use *in these uncertain times* in the first line of every email. The phrase was everywhere all of a sudden, a chorus. Between March and June, by some estimates, media use of the phrase *new normal* increased by 759 per cent.

Every time I hear the words *new normal* I feel a recoil, swift and small and deep within my belly. I hate how normal we find the idea of normal, how many other narratives and experiences and people it excludes and elides and diminishes. I hate how often it's assumed that normal is something we only ever choose not to be, rather than something that rejects us regardless of whether or not (and consciously or not) we try to mould ourselves to fit. And I hated, at the beginning of the pandemic, how each time I heard the phrase the only thing that I could think was this:

For me, *new normal* is old news.

—

It was close to a full decade ago when someone first said the words *new normal* to me. They were said by the dietitian who ran the first hospital programme I ever attended, towards the end of one of the many frustrating conversations I'd tried to have there with her – her main tactic for dealing with any kind of questioning or dissent was to pretend it wasn't happening at all. It's just *not normal,* I'd eventually spluttered, trying to explain how difficult I was finding keeping to all of the elaborate and exacting rules of my meal plan. This is your *new normal,* she'd very calmly returned, and insisted that as such, it was a thing that I had to get used to.

In hindsight, there's something a bit spurious in the way the dietitian said this – the *new normal* she was suggesting, those pre-planned and perfectly timed set portions and specific combinations of food, that incredibly systematised and ordered pattern of eating was also, I was repeatedly told, intended as a stopgap measure, a way to retrain my body and brain until these healthier habits were so well entrenched that I could start to bend and break the rules without them disappearing entirely. *New normal* was a stepping stone to *normal eating*. It would give way again to normal. *New normal* wasn't something I was supposed to need forever.

Except that it was, and it is; and slowly coming to understand that my *new normal* was one of lasting illness, of endless small concessions and adjustments, and that this wasn't tragic or a failure to recover, but a way of living that was pragmatic, practical, kind – this, more than anything else, was what helped me regain my sense of agency and adequacy and to feel less ill within my illness.

—

Sometimes I think that what made the difference for me last year was that my being so unused to regularity, to anything that isn't unpredictable or precarious, meant that when these things suddenly fell away, when the world for so many people became uncomfortable, unreliable, unstable, it didn't feel all that different for me. More often, I think it's because I first felt that shock of vulnerability, that realisation that my body was always subject to forces that I could not control or predict, close to two decades ago. It was bewildering and terrifying and a destabilisation that I felt at my fundament, my core. It took me years to come to terms with this; and the pandemic granted no one else this luxury of time.

Last year, I felt equipped. I've understood the precarity of my body and the limits of what it can be exposed to for years; I've had to moderate what I want to do with what I'm physically able to do for just as long. I've been isolated and lonely all my life. I already worked from home. None of these things needed adjustment.

Early on, once the initial shock, that first wave of anxiety and wild speculation and fear had passed – I felt these as much as any other person, and am not pretending otherwise – I remember being startled by my new congruence with the world, the way that so many people were finding difficult the parts of my life that only now feel unremarkable to me. This too is something to which I'm unaccustomed: my experiences don't often fit the narratives that are told about our world, what we can expect within and from it. But neither did the pandemic – which is why we had no way to understand it, nothing to measure or map it against, no way yet to find its meaning.

The media kept calling it unprecedented, even though it wasn't

– we'd just forgotten or ignored those parts of our history, looked away from those parts of the world.

I felt like a precedent. *New normal* looked so much like my existing normal, and I wanted to tell everyone that they would be okay. That it would hurt, a lot, but eventually they would be okay.

—

My girlfriend talks a lot about the idea of normal, both in conversation and for her work. In part this is because her two main fields – technology and design – are disciplines in which assumptions about normal behaviours and normal desires underpin everything that is done (and are often responsible for some of their biggest mistakes). And in part this is because she too has never fitted within the boundaries of normal, much as she once tried, and because she was forced to abandon the attempt years before I could. Her more comfortable, although still incomplete, acceptance of this was a revelation to me when we first met. Normal, she always says, is a simple mathematical term. It is the measure that accounts for everything that sits beneath the steeply sloped part of a bell curve, the part that rings the loudest when you strike it. Normal, she always says, really just means common. It doesn't mean standard, or regular, or natural, or any variety of good; just as it doesn't mean boring or simple or bad – all it means is that there's a lot of it around. But even as a mathematical measure, normal always excludes around 30 per cent of any sample – which is a huge amount, no matter how you look at it. *New normal,* whatever it might look like, must inevitably do this too.

—

My work doesn't depend on hospitality or service or performance, and so it didn't shut down entirely; nor is it low-paid or precarious enough that I would have had to turn up even if I were sick. I don't live with children who would have needed home-schooling or care; I wasn't stranded in a country where I was not a citizen and couldn't access government support. I wasn't separated from my family and friends, or facing eviction. No one I love was ever in immediate risk. I know I'm lucky, that even as my illness made me both more vulnerable to the virus and better trained to live with its restrictions, there were so many people who suffered, who suffer still. I watched the news and the numbers from overseas and interstate, and couldn't shake the sense that my good fortune was as outrageous as it was entirely accidental.

—

I've been trying to work out how many years it has been, now, that I have been working from home, counting backwards through the different houses that I've set up beds and desks in, all of my different jobs and roles. But I can't do it, can't seem to figure out exactly when it was that I began – and that's because, I realise, aside from an ill-fated three-month stint in my first job straight out of uni (my girlfriend insists this doesn't count because it was with a theatre company), as an adult I have always worked in this way.

I've worked from home after my shifts and on the days that I had off from crappy part-time jobs and I've worked from home for small and new and sometimes loosely tied organisations where every employee worked remotely. I've taught casually in universities, driving in for few-hour blocks of classes once or twice each week. There have been piecemeal contracts and one-off workshops and self-employment, and across it all, the work of writing. For as long as I've been working I have been working from home, from a desk beneath a window in a sharehouse bedroom, and entirely alone.

I like working from home. I've always said this, and as the years have passed it has slowly become more wholly true. Each time I walk into an office building I'm confounded by how artificial and airless they always seem, how many people exist there together, without having anything in common except for their shared space. I can't settle in these buildings, always feel itchy and on edge – it's only recently that I have realised how common this is for autistic people (*new normal*). An office never really was an option, although I obviously didn't know that when I first started working from home. In those early years, I didn't know a single other person who also worked out of their home. It can't have been that rare a situation, I know now, even though the full power of the internet for opening up small businesses and crafty cottage industries run out of peoples' kitchens had not yet been realised. Working from home just wasn't something that people in my world, from my world – suburban, practical, sensible-jobbed – ever did. (Yes, I'm talking about class.)

What I'm saying here is, I had no model of how to do it. I was young, and still ferociously determined; already unwell but years away from knowing it. I threw myself into my work, despite having no idea of how to manage it in these conditions but also as a way to try to cope with these conditions by refusing them entirely. I worked full, long days without real breaks; sometimes several of these would pass without my speaking to another living creature. I hustled, although that word was not in common usage yet, often worked on three or four (at one time, seven) different projects or contracts simultaneously. I know what I was thinking, always, was *this has been my choice.* This was what it meant to try to write as a profession, to work without so many of the structures and the safety of the regular working world, this was what I had to do to make it work. *I chose this*, I kept thinking, and so I had to make it work. I had to find a way to make it work.

—

The most useful, most damning, story about *normal* I've ever encountered, comes from design – a now-famous cautionary tale taken from the US Air Force in the wake of the Second World War. When designing the cockpits of their new jet fighter planes, the military engineers drew on the country's enlistment records – medical histories which included for each recruit an extensive series of body measurements (the obvious ones, but also things like thumb length, the distance from eye to ear, circumference of the ankle, neck and wrist). It was a vast database, and one that was perfect, the engineers thought, for ensuring that the small cockpit space would best fit the average pilot who might sit there.

But the results were disastrous – which is to say, the planes kept crashing at a truly spectacular rate– because even within this already fairly homogenous sample (all men, all relatively healthy, and all under six feet tall, a requirement for pilots at the time) not a single person actually matched that average, that determined normal. Not a single person could easily or comfortably manoeuvre all of the controls, because none of their bodies individually fitted the standard that had been determined from them collectively. The design was soon amended to include adjustable seats and levers and steering wheels – and the accident rate dropped immediately.

(The same, incidentally, is true of cars – when all of these fixtures were indeed fixed in place, women had far more accidents than men, for whose bodies cars were originally designed; since these have been adjustable, the reverse has proven to be true.)

Some designers call this kind of misapprehension 'the flaw of averages'; I know the reason that I like this particular idea so much is because so many one-size devices don't account for people my size – the automatic doors that don't open for me unless I approach them dead-centre or wave my hands above my head and into their sensors' reach, the sunshades in my car that don't quite keep the afternoon light from my eyes unless I stretch my back and crane my neck and all but lift up from the seat. For how much of the made world doesn't fit me either: the comfortably cool cinemas (and offices) that I shiver in, the cheerfully lit shopping centres that blur my brain, the generous portions in restaurants that so easily bring me to panic: all of these averages and normals that constantly remind me of what I'm not.

—

Over the years, I did find a way to make my means of working work, to build routines to shape my days, to be gentler with myself on the days that felt stodgy, and to seek out small interactions when my mouth and tongue felt stiff with disuse. I got a dog, and it was only when I found myself continually surprised by her continual soft presence by my side that I even noticed how lonely I had been. Against it all, that constant drumbeat: I chose this, and so I have to make it work. I chose this, so I am not allowed to complain.

At the beginning of the pandemic, both of my housemates worked in governmental offices that shut down suddenly, and over one weekend they set up their clunky laptops in their bedrooms, one of them on top of a trestle table because she'd never had – and never needed – her own desk. It felt like the transition happened overnight, and in the first weeks especially they were drifty and skittish, surprised by how the days all felt so long. One cooked elaborate lunches with multiple ingredients and many-step prep; the other did load after load of washing. There was a lot of online shopping. We intercepted each other on the staircase and outside the bathroom, and destroyed our internet connection one morning by joining three separate Zoom meetings at the same time.

In the media and on the socials, people were joking about no longer needing shoes or bras, or despairing about their stir-craziness, their boredom, the way their days seemed to melt together. I don't know how I'm supposed to focus, one of my housemates said, I don't know what I am supposed to do.

It took me some time to realise it, but I took great solace in this. A strange and not uncomplicated solace, but a deep one nonetheless, in how difficult my housemates and my friends, the wider world, was suddenly finding the everyday conditions of my life. It was working from home that made this obvious – when everybody around me started talking about the shapelessness, the isolation, all of that time in one's own brain, how there's no way to diffuse any small madness or emotion that might build across the day. I felt something lift within me. I hadn't quite been able to admit that working in this way was hard (I chose this), didn't quite believe in this difficulty when I'd only felt it in myself. I'd seen it only as my own weakness, some kind of flimsiness of self. I didn't know I needed this reassurance until that small but somehow deeply felt nugget of blame fell away.

So much of the pandemic felt like this to me. Time and time again, I saw so many people struggling in so many small ways to adapt to the way I've had to live my life for so long. I kept remembering how much of an upheaval it had been to become ill, to adjust to this, but also how determined I had been to keep on keeping on, to grit my teeth, to not complain. So much of the pandemic, for me, was validating in this way, and I was heartened.

I've never felt so comfortable in my life.

—

One of the strangest things about the idea of normal is how often people tell me they don't care about the idea of normal. And that I shouldn't either, because normal isn't important, isn't real, doesn't matter. It's not that I disagree, more that I think so many of us do care, even or especially as we protest the opposite. It's hard not to, given that it's always all around us. I didn't think that I cared either, until recently – but this, for me at least, was the revelatory power of my autism diagnosis. The very definition of neurodivergence, as a category and a term, is that it is not typical, not the norm. It is a diagnosis that says, yes, you are different; yes, your brain doesn't operate in the usual way – and as such, it makes sense of so much of the confusion and diffused hurt, that bruisedness, that I have felt for so much of my life.

Many psychologists account for the much higher rates of mental illness in autistic people (especially in those diagnosed late, like me) by claiming this as the toll of trying – and constantly failing – to fit to social norms and pressures that are unspoken and unexplained and only really evident when you get them wrong. No person deliberately exerts these pressures. The abrasions that are caused are small. They're often hard to notice at the time, but they happen again and again, relentlessly and unceasingly, and it doesn't take long to feel yourself entirely skinless. It's difficult to experience this across an entire lifetime and not think yourself at fault.

By this reckoning, it sometimes seems to me that it may very well have been the idea of normal that caused the problem, led to my illness, in the first place. How constantly and keenly I felt myself to sit outside of normal, how I never knew how to inhabit whatever options might be left to me. How I couldn't seem to figure out or follow the rules that operate in the world, and so developed some of my own, iron-clad and fierce, in the hope that they might contain me instead.

Neurodivergence is framed differently to illness: it is not a problem, not something that could or should be solved or cured. Instead, what it requires is adjustment (*new normal*) and understanding, a gentleness that I'm still learning to reach for. In a way, I taught myself to do this before I knew precisely why it was so necessary, to stop pushing myself beyond my limits and reaching for normal-looking things that I never could attain. I had no model for how to do it, but I found a way to make it work.

—

The solace I felt when the people around me were struggling to adjust to working from home, however, was always tinted with frustration, because I know too that it's only because I've always been able to work from home that I have been able to work – consistently, even at all – across the long duration of my illness. I have so many disabled friends who've had to leave their jobs, or the workforce entirely, because their employers wouldn't grant them these conditions, as if it were the office itself that were the work, rather than whatever it is that happens inside of it, or some kind of physical supervision or crowd censure is needed for adults to actually do the tasks they are paid to complete.

Disabled people have been asking for workplace flexibility for years, for our employers to grant us the 'reasonable adjustments', and the autonomy – to say nothing of dignity – not to have to try and fit into spaces and routines and interactions that cause us harm, if they are even possible at all. The technology for remote access to intranets and email and tele- or video-conferencing has been around for even longer. When the pandemic hit, it felt like these concessions were granted universally, immediately, and without fuss – but only because it was now able-bodied people, *normal* people, who needed them. I don't think any employer found this simple – but it certainly wasn't as difficult, impossible, as they'd been telling us it would be.

It was barely a week later that the government 'supplemented' its income support payments across the pandemic, in the first real increase to these payments in twenty-six years. Ineligible for the supplement, though, were people whose unemployment preceded the pandemic, and those on disability support (the 'undeserving poor,' as some sections of the media dubbed them). In the months that followed, doctors and specialists were suddenly allowed to practise telehealth, holding appointments over the phone or via Zoom – where previously, and inexplicably, these kinds of appointments were ineligible for Medicare subsidies (I couldn't help but think of how much this would have helped me when I had two or three such appointments every week and walked the route to every single one of them). The number of subsidised psychology sessions available each year was doubled. Allowances for extra sick leave were made by many employers (though this was unmandated and far from universal). I'm certainly not the only disabled person who was infuriated by this – not by the provisions themselves, which are so welcome and so needed, but for how long they'd been denied to us, deemed unnecessary.

What it made me realise was that until this physical precarity affected the wider world, the wider world had not seen me as fully human, as worthy of this kind of care.

—

By April, my house was suddenly far less empty, far less quiet than I was used to. And this was my biggest adjustment last year: my working conditions became more social, full of people at a time when so many people were adapting to being far more on their own. I liked the casual kindliness of this, the way that there was always and immediately someone close at hand whenever the fraught emotions of that time overtook any one of us, the way we added to our routines a shared morning coffee run, a weekly afternoon dance-off in the front room that also involved singing along at the top of our lungs (and for which I started dressing up in increasingly glittery outfits, just because I could). But despite this, I couldn't help but feel unsettled, distracted, newly conscious of my movements and habits, my space.

I felt the loss of my solitude, that is, and I felt it deeply. All the more so once I started seeing so many news articles about combatting loneliness, about the phenomenon of skin hunger, that profound and painful longing for physical touch in times of isolation – and wondering what it was about me that so ached for the opposite.

Within weeks, I started shoving the essentials of my workplace – my laptop, my two notebooks, a folder full of research, books – into a backpack and carrying them to my girlfriend's house, ten minutes' walk away. It wasn't technically legal – the restrictions at the time did allow people to visit their partner, but neither of us would have come close to using that word at that time. But because she lived alone, and because she is also chronically unwell, and had only recently been discharged from a hospitalisation, we figured we could call it 'caring duties' if the question were ever asked.

So this is how I worked across the lockdown: at my girlfriend's desk or on her couch or on the outdoor setting in her garden that she'd draped with velvet and lace netting to soften the dark concrete the whole space was spackled with. We'd alternate between these three locations, the desk taken up by whoever was on a call or teaching or recording; we learnt that if we timed our afternoon coffee run for 3 p.m., the café on the corner was likely to palm off its leftover pastries for free. But we did all of this cautiously, especially at first, both of us nervous about sharing so much space so frequently. My girlfriend too was used to working from home and to being almost entirely on her own; she too treasures her silence, and is reticent with the parts of herself that feel awkward or difficult and unshareable. She too didn't think herself cut out for this, and so I know that we were both surprised, and even shaken, by how easy and how lovely we quickly found it to be, working alone, together. I don't think either of us ever thought it possible. We live together now, in a different house almost equidistant from each of our old homes, our books comingled (but alphabetised) across our shelves. Without the pandemic, I'm certain this would not have happened.

—

It was from this space – sitting at my girlfriend's desk in the corner of her living room – that I attended my first online book launch, one that was hosted by my local bookshop over Zoom. Technically, I was working: I was interviewing the author, who had originally intended to fly to Sydney for the occasion, but now sat in front of her bookshelves with a lanky greyhound curled up on a couch somewhere to her side. None of this is remarkable, not anymore; but what was wonderful that night, what felt thrilling and precious, was watching, as the event kicked off, the names of the people who were attending light up across the screen. The launch was for Katerina Bryant's book about disability, invisible illness and hysteria across history, the lives of women these have affected; and what I rapidly and joyfully realised was that so many of the attendees were people who I recognise, I know, from Twitter. Out in force was so much of the community that has formed there, of and for disabled writers and readers – Literary Disability Twitter, as it were. Being together like this isn't something that we're *normally* able to do: not only do we live in different cities and different states, but so many of us so often aren't able to take our bodies or brains to an in-person event. The joy in the room, even without there being a room, was palpable, the energy as well. I buzzed with this for hours.

It was only later that I realised that this kind of gathering never should have been a rarity, something exceptional and so thrilling. It's been possible for us to be together like this – just as it's been possible for our workplaces to be flexible – for years. For years it should have been this way, and the fact that it hasn't is a tragedy.

—

Once I'd settled into this new routine, this new space, my work last year was largely uninterrupted. If anything, I was busier than usual, having taken on some extra teaching at a different university (where I had to fight to be able to continue to teach online, because their return-to-campus exemptions were only available for permanent staff). I know these circumstances were unusual, that continuing on like this, largely untouched, was as rare as it was profoundly fortunate. The sole reason I am mentioning this is because it's only now, almost midway through 2021, that I've found myself foundering.

Suddenly, with the worst of the pandemic most likely behind us, in this country at least, and with our lives quickly 'opening back up' (another phrase that doesn't sit that comfortably with me, given that there was never anything closed about my more cautious existence) my work has started to feel difficult, overwhelming. I can't concentrate, or focus long enough to write in anything other than fits and starts. I can't seem to stay organised, to feel like I'm keeping up (and I'm certainly not getting ahead); the way my email would be piling up if it had physical form is terrifying. I'm reading less. There just isn't enough time. Last year, I would have shrugged all of this off, as a very natural response to upheaval and uncertainty and disruption and doubt, to *these unprecedented times*. I would have felt myself to be in a very normal boat, all of us rowing together (*we're all in this together,* after all).

This year, it's the return to normal that I'm finding hard. It doesn't feel like there's more work, or that it's spread more thinly, or that anything practical or quantifiable has changed. It's more that I'm not ready to readjust, to go back to a normal that never suited me all that well. I don't want the world not to have changed. I can't bear for the world not to have changed.

—

It was at the end of March last year that Scott Morrison first used the word *snapback*. I hardly noticed it at the time, in no small part, I think, because so much of the reporting, even when it touched directly on this, still used the phrase *new normal* in its headlines. But Morrison hardly ever said *new normal* – I can only find the phrase appearing once in government documents and announcements from last year – because a *new normal* isn't something he ever had any interest in. Instead, Morrison has insisted that there will be a *snapback*, a quick return to regularity; and the first time he did so was mere days after his government announced its programme of pandemic-response support. That supplement to the dole (but not the DSP), those JobKeeper payments for struggling businesses (as long as they weren't universities or arts companies or employers of short-term casuals), the free childcare, extra Medicare benefits, eviction moratorium, emergency access to superannuation – none of these, he said, should be considered a *new normal*, none of these would last. It was *snapback* that was the plan; *snapback* to the old normal and to business as usual that we should hope for and expect.

But I don't want to go back, snappily or otherwise. I don't want the world not to have changed. I enjoyed my brief congruence with the world; I enjoyed having my needs met and understood, the rare privilege of feeling typical and un-alone. And having to relinquish that once again, having to hand back over that consideration of my full humanity, feels nothing less than cruel.

In the opening page of *Illness as Metaphor*, Susan Sontag writes that alongside our regular world exists a 'kingdom of the sick', one for which we all hold 'dual citizenship', even as we deny this fact for as long and as often as we can. During the pandemic, it felt like the entire population came to inhabit this kingdom, to live alongside me and according to its customs and laws, those which have shaped my life for so long. A lot of people liked it here, I know this, even as so many more felt homesick and couldn't wait to return. I think I let myself forget that it wasn't a migration I was witnessing, but just a brief and very busy tourist season. But I don't have an exit visa; I can't ever return to the kingdom of the well. I know I'm going to be left behind, can feel it happening already, once again. It's difficult to have to grieve this all over, once more, to have my normal and my world so vehemently rejected, once again, to watch on as wider society refuses to adapt for people like me, or to change.

The Ten Thousand Things

Suneeta Peres da Costa

1

The bag of drugs is sitting untouched on the kitchen bench beside the cans of diced tomatoes and chickpeas I'd earlier quarantined. They – cans not drugs – may be useful, I think, although in less apocalyptic times, *I might prefer* to soak dried chickpeas to make hummus or chana masala. The chickpea glut follows a 9 p.m. masked assault of Harris Farm Leichhardt and the fact the ex has recently turned up unannounced with a care package of more canned pulses, organic brown rice and greens than I have room to store. An Amma devotee never known to hug spontaneously, he'd stood at the mandated distance of one Kylie Minogue on the other side of my gate (less gateless gate than gate that never shuts properly, the broken latch, I observed as he handed me the box, one of the ten thousand things now unlikely to be repaired...).

I hadn't the heart to tell him I already had enough chickpeas. Long before lockdown, I noticed he'd developed the habit of addressing me in the third person – as in, 'How is Suneeta?' – but this now felt part of the new protocol, a kind of quarantining, albeit voluntary, too. Was there anything else I needed? 'Actually, there was...', I started. At one time I would have settled for his child but now, the wit, said, 'your urine'. Deadpan, I added the citrus needed to be fertilised with testosterone and, as I didn't want to risk going to Bunnings, would be glad if he could oblige. He walked away muttering, 'you've got to be joking', but I called after him that I was serious; he could at least fill a few old milk bottles...? It would soon be my birthday and I hoped he'd come through! Afterwards, I went out the back to inspect the intensity of the lime tree's anaemia. A familiar pain sliced through my abdomen and, the better to distract myself, I leaned in and hugged the paperbark.

The friend who knows about the drugs calls to remind me to check the expiry dates; she has gone through many gruelling and exorbitant cycles herself. She tells me, sotto voce, that she might have to be redeployed. It has been years since she has worked as a nurse, but she has been called up now, enlisted. In a show of solidarity and friendly reassurance, I unhelpfully exclaim, 'Oh, Gawd!' For the next few moments neither of us says anything; all I hear is the faint rise and fall of her breath on the other side of the phone. We hang up and I briefly, bracingly, open the cooler bag. It is filled with brand new hypodermic needles, a plethora of antiseptic rubs and a small sharps bin that has been meticulously included. I am agile and creative, earmarking, as if for a war effort, how these could be repurposed. Perhaps I too could join the frontline by at the very least giving myself (or another, should they trust me) a flu shot? Pass them on to some diabetics I know?

I am supposed to be writing this essay, ostensibly on technology, but am distracted, enervated, channelling Pompey Casmilus who, convalescing from Freddy heartbreak, office doldrums and friendship ennui, travels on doctor's orders to a Schloss on the Baltic coast in Stevie Smith's *Over the Frontier*. It's the very eve of the second world war and she who confesses to being afraid of needles ('Pompey very very bad soldier') is suddenly awoken to Allied duty:

> Oh war war is all my thought. And suddenly I am very alert and not dreaming now asleep at all, but very awake and for ever more, and not

dreaming again at all [...] but very practical I am become. Achtung, achtung! I hope that I am very practical.

But, caught in the freakish time warp of a new world order, I feel I could equally be, fleeing Shen Fever and holed up in a mall outside of Chicago with protagonist Candace Chen, in Ling Ma's prophetic, post-apocalyptic novel, *Severance*:

Our Googlings darkened, turned inward. We Googled *maslow's pyramid* to see how many of the need levels we could already fulfill [...] we Googled *7 stages grief* to track our emotional progress. We were at Anger, the slower among us lagging behind at Denial. We Googled *is there a god*, clicked *I'm Feeling Lucky*, and were directed to a suicide hotline site.

But actually, no, I am in my kitchen in Sydney. The ice pack has perforated and is oozing its freezing liquid. As luck would have it, the fridge is leaking too (*another* of the ten thousand things...). The drugs themselves, having languished through the long, apocalyptic summer (is this a double apocalypse?), have names like Cetrotide and Orgalutran, which I can't help notice are near-anagrams of, respectively, ecocide and gargantuan. Made in France or Germany, without the Pharmaceutical Benefits Scheme they'd have set me back at least $700. If I squint I can see the instructions say to store them between two and eight degrees Celsius and, stamped in bigger letters across the cooler bag, the following warning: 'NOT designed to keep your medicines at the required storage temperature'. *Whereas*, I console myself, concerned with different economies of scale, *the chickpeas were just $1.99 organic*. I place them, earliest-to-latest expiration date, in the pantry drawer, momentarily soothed by this most humdrum of housekeeping enterprises.

2

It is within these interstices of consciousness, existential intentions stripped to questions of contagion, to sheer utilitarianism, that thought – *if thought it can be called* – alights in those first days, weeks and even months, but there are also blind spots and dead ends where it does not move at all, corners where it collides with dust balls or becomes entangled with ever-lengthening, ever-greying hair – *Whose! Mine?* – on the floorboards. *I am supposed to be writing this essay, ostensibly on technology*, but the rooms of the house become a labyrinth, a game of snakes and ladders, a ten-thousand-piece jigsaw puzzle in which I am apt to forget my task or purpose. It's like *No Exit*, except that Hell is now Self as much as Other People. Marooned in ruminative cul-de-sacs, hide-outs, cubbyholes, the Inner Child tumbles in too. Sullen when I refuse to play with her, she acts up, acts out. By day she moves far away from me, to return at 3 a.m. to disturb my already fitful sleep.

When I wake it is to snags of fear which I anxiously ravel and unravel in the manner of some very weird Penelopiad. Against Prime Ministerial advice, I cower from the cascade of woeful planetary realities and creep further under the doona. I decidedly *don't want* to be found and so don't bother to install the tracing app. The Inner Critic nevertheless discovers me malingering and asks, *Inner Child, Suneeta? Yes*, I obediently answer. *Like an Imaginary Friend? Yes*, I aver. *A Jungian Fantasy! Probably the result of a regressive ego doing service for the child you will never have. HaHAhaHA!* Indeed, perhaps the only evidence of time passing will be my own extinction, my toenails growing intolerably long, scraping the bedsheet. Or the susurration, the white noise, of someone washing their hands and singing 'Happy Birthday to You', revealed in the streaky bathroom mirror to be none other than me, myself and I.

When a prospective employer contacts me to discuss a job I've almost forgotten I interviewed for, there are ten thousand tabs open on my browser and I may accidently hit 'share screen'. I pretend to be adapting well to the new technology, although such is my self-consciousness that, at least under my breath, I have taken to calling Zoom Zoo instead. Answering emails or texts, white space engulfs all known signifiers. I type like a demon, like my life depends on it, like I'm breaking a code – but omitting whole letters and words, drop into a deeper disquiet about whether things will still exist if communication is also leaky; could we subjects fall in, slip through, dematerialise? Reading, the mind finds no traction or narrative hold, instead rehearsing doom-saying lines it learned by rote long ago from 'The Second Coming', 'Prufrock' and *Lear*. It hesitates, procrastinates; its imaginative leaps and exploits extend no further than making a found poem, a zootic petition of sorts, from Marianne Moore's 'Pangolin':

near artichoke,
mammal unpugnacious,
modest spruce-cone,
unemotional armored animal,
true ant-eater, not cockroach-eater –
draw away from danger...

I am supposed to be writing this essay, ostensibly on technology, but not for the first time, I believe I am unable to write; and not writing, doubt that I will ever write again. I wonder whether such a loss will even be noticed, will matter even less now than any time before, given relative prospects of dying from an incurable virus, annihilating the planet, or being swallowed whole by the algorithm – none of which can any longer be called 'catastrophising'. In any event, Arundhati Roy, in her searing essay 'The Pandemic is a Portal', may have already said it for me and you too:

> Who can use the term 'gone viral' now without shuddering a little? Who can look at anything any more – a door handle, a cardboard carton, a bag of vegetables – without imagining it swarming with those unseeable, undead, unliving blobs dotted with suction pads waiting to fasten themselves on to our lungs? Who can think of kissing a stranger, jumping on to a bus or sending their child to school without feeling real fear? Who can think of ordinary pleasure and not assess its risk?

3

I am supposed to be writing this essay, ostensibly on technology, but the phone keeps vibrating. It is a sibling texting updates about the fate of an elderly relative who, found near-dead in her apartment at the beginning of lockdown, has just come out of ICU. I am devastated to learn she had given advance care directives to have life support turned off. She has no mobile and I am terrified of going to visit her. When I call, the nurses pass her the ward phone and I quarantine information about the outside world – until the phone itself is identified as a possible source of contagion. I hurry off, as though this may forestall harm, but she tells me not to worry, that Jesus is protecting us. Later, she is transferred to a mental hospital where she chatters away on a phone all patients can, randomly, use as much as they like; she tells me she's playing the piano, tunes of her youth – 'My Bonnie Lies Over the Ocean', 'Johnnie's So Long at the Fair', 'When Irish Eyes Are Smiling'. When I promise to visit she thinks it's a party and asks me to bring the junk food she's craving. I envy her her delusions.

Ordinarily a sceptic, I am nevertheless so lonely waiting for the world to end that I find myself wading into the social media slipstream, blithely retweeting quarantine music made by Italians from their apartment windows and balconies. Some are singing the anti-fascist anthem 'Bella Ciao'; one poignantly serenades his Sicilian neighbours with 'Imagine' on a sax. Soon a bunch of A-list Hollywood actors are accused of bastardising this same song from the comfort of their Hollywood Hills villas; and, however murky, I confess to stepping into the same river twice, hopeful of encountering Mark Ruffalo on his sofa. Speaking of polluted waterways, it seems the Venetian canals have now cleared up; one can even see dolphins swimming in them! Oh, but no, no, no! It was all a bit of beguiling photoshopping, magical thinking, a hoax, #FakeNews! The ex sends a cosmic joke horoscope that has been making the rounds; each star sign is greeted by the same facetious forecast: 'You'll be spending time in your home'.

My dad sends the same joke along with other, at times politically incorrect, jokes on WhatsApp. One of these includes a skit of a smug Indian school teacher taking class attendance in the year 2025: 'Quarantina Joshi, Lockdown Singh, Social Distance Singh…'. The punchline involves a boy called Covid Awasthi who has been truant, whom she scolds, 'Covid, pay attention in class or I will send you back to China!'. Meanwhile, three of Jammu and Kashmir's Associated Press photographers win the Pulitzer Prize for their feature pictures of Kashmir's lockdown since the Revocation of Article 370 of India's Constitution on 5 August 2019. In the most militarised place on earth, under cover of the pandemic, the Indian Army has upped the scale of its surveillance and control of the Kashmiri population: extending a communications blackout, raising the homes of suspected 'terrorists'. Overnight, 'domicile' laws have also been introduced which, like the citizenship amendments of late 2019, threaten the sovereignty of the local Muslim population (who in this case form the majority).

I retweet Mukhtar Khan's prize-winning photograph of six-year-old Muneefa Nazir 'whose right eye was hit by a marble allegedly shot by Indian Paramilitary soldiers'; then, some hours later, unable to sleep, come downstairs to find I have several new 'followers' I don't recognise, seemingly also followers of senior members of India's ruling party...Dad also sends a mash-up of the harrowing scenes this side of the Line of Actual Control when, following four hours' notice of lockdown introduced by the Prime Minister, Narendra Modi, millions of itinerant migrant workers pour out of Indian cities, hitching rides on super-spreading, crowded trucks, cycling or walking home for days, children carrying their elderly parents on their backs. Bereft of house-help, multitudes of the urban middle class turn out to give the workers a tone-deaf send-off, bashing pots and pans on their balconies in a manner more la brutta figura than bella ciao. Workers who remain behind breaking restrictions are given humiliating corporeal punishments like sit-ups, push-ups or beaten with lathis by police patrolling city streets.

Ivanka Trump is trolled for lauding the 'beautiful feat of endurance and love' of fifteen-year-old Jyoti Kumari who cycles home to Bihar with her disabled father on the back of her bicycle. I wonder under what circumstances she or I would carry our fathers? I talk to my friend, an American citizen of Indian origin, who lives with her partner in Gurugram, where Jyoti's father had an autorickshaw business. We discuss the dark side of endurance and love, otherwise known as starvation and death; the role of daughters in the Indian family system, and the paradox that punishment for untouchability – a concept central to both Brahminism and Hindutva ideology – could prove a more virulent scourge than Covid-19. We discuss the lies at the heart of the phrases, 'world's biggest democracy' and 'richest country in the world'. My friend has had to let her cook go for a time, and we exchange recipes for chutney and dosa batter; we show each other how long our hair has grown and, beyond the frame of the camera, she gestures to the dogs who are hungrier and the park where she longs to walk, except for curfew and the monkeys who've grown boisterous.

All the same, Sadhguru's prophesying it will all be over soon, he has a gut feeling (though cautions about eating meat). The important thing is to keep calm, not let your mind be disturbed! Certainly do not confuse self-isolation with discrimination! Sensible people I know join the becalming ranks of a #WarandPeace reading group while I frantically refresh my *Guardian Australia* feed which, at any given moment, may reveal strikes of international Amazon workers; a locust plague threatening the entire cereal crop in the Horn of Africa, and the allegorical tale of the two Coopers in New York's Central Park. *I am supposed to be writing this essay, ostensibly on technology*, but one day in late May it is reported that Rio Tinto has blown up the ancient rock shelters of the Juukan Gorge. Just a few days later, a video goes viral of a black man in Minneapolis who, on suspicion of buying a packet of cigarettes with a counterfeit twenty-dollar bill, is suffocated to death by the police who arrest him.

4

My period is late and then I start to bleed profusely. My face also hurts. When I report my distress to a friend, a poet, she asks have I been grinding my teeth. There's a good chance I've been gnashing them, I say – and I'm not referring to the literary fiasco that has erupted online in which she, I and everyone else we know appear to be implicated by mere association. It's my frontal lobe that ails me, I say, *as though it might be ossifying*. 'Horn or tusk?' she clarifies. We begin to speculate about rhinos and narwhals and before I can answer which, she suggests, 'Suneeta, perhaps you're turning into a unicorn?'. We burst into hysterical laughter and I feel a fleeting, creaturely limbering, a forgetfulness, an ease. As though proof of Levinas' ethics, the muscles of my face, so tense till now, suddenly release. Yet the moment is also inflected with the tenuousness of our promise to see each other soon, the realisation now, more than ever, that the ten thousand things are completely evanescent, unable to be captured in words on screen, far less by emoji, however cute or pithy: 🦄🖤🖤🖤

I've left ten thousand messages on my mother's answering machine and sent as many texts telling her to please refrain from shopping in crowded malls, taking public transport, going to mass, to restaurants, etc. I can get her groceries or do errands on her behalf. No answer, no answer, no answer. One afternoon, when I have learnt to be okay with the silence, that I have done my part, my daughterly duty, Mum arrives as an unmasked ghost at my door. Letting her in cautiously, I ask how she has come? By public transport, she tells me. *Covid-19 is not contagious!* With infinite forbearance, I go into the kitchen, make her a cuppa, citing a few statistics – Kawasaki's syndrome, the UK death toll that day – but it's too late, she's picking up her bag and already moving towards the door. Summoning her back is futile. At the same time, some primal force arises in the Inner Child, a biological tug of war, that compels her/me to follow. It feels like an ancient ritual, a primordial dance: her/me waiting for the lights; her/my heart palpitating; she/me crossing the road, putting herself/myself in harm's way in a quest to ferry my mother a spare face mask. But she disappears into the train station, which may as well be the River Lethe...

'The nameless is the mother of heaven and earth. The named is the mother of the ten thousand things'; *I'm supposed to be writing this essay on technology*, but I'm reading the *Tao Te Ching*. Where does heaven leave off from earth, dream from waking and life from death? Does poetry remake the world by transfiguring our suffering, our grief? Should we, as Adam Zagajewski exhorts, '[p]raise the mutilated world/[...] and the gentle light that strays and vanishes/and returns'? Is there, even in sundering, a grace, as in Ali Cobby Eckermann's 'Dip':

my mother is playing hide and seek
between my memory and my dreams
....

no longer foetal I must arise
no longer prone she has arisen

No doubt the Bard himself, who lived through plague, was prescient to have asked,

What's yet in this
That bears the name of life? Yet in this life
Lie hid moe thousand deaths: yet death we fear,
That makes these odds all even.

I read April Bernard's 'Haunt', in which the speaker is attended by the ghost of her recently departed mother, a poem that lifts and carries me through that particularly trying week:

There she is, darkening
my starboard periphery un-
smiling, reaching cold mist hands
into mine to whisk the eggs, fold
the sheets, sort the papers, choose
spools of thread for stitching
another face mask. This is her kind
of catastrophe, rife with irony and fear

The sky hangs as though held up by scaffolding; the trees sway on their hinges; the birds, eerily quiet, seem part of an artificial set, except for the fragile, faded chalk drawings of neighbourhood children that include rainbows and the longest hopscotches I've ever seen. When it rains, the kids remake them the next sunny day and I'm touched by these small, irrepressible acts of faith in the quotidian. For a wild moment they seem a throwback to a time when the boundaries between inside and outside, self and other, were softer, more porous; indeed, a time when I was still young myself. Though I feel my age and childlessness most particularly now, this evolutionary logic – the one true and ultimate TikTok – is counterpointed by a deep ambivalence about bringing children into, and a helpless rage about, the fate of this ravaged world and the broken planetary covenant, the legacy of waste and destruction which is being left to future generations.

(Yet perhaps I am being overly sentimental for in 'normal times' hopscotches are in fact as rare a sight as the children who now find them a release from being cooped up and home-schooled during the aberration of lockdown. In 'normal times' the children are, like me, often voluntary prisoners of their screens. In a country like Australia, with comparatively high levels of freedom of speech and democratic rule of law, there's a paradox to our technological enchainment and enslavement. That social media is disrupting, corrupting and distorting our relationships with ourselves and others, fracturing and fragmenting our psyches, polity and public sphere, has been well-observed. And we ourselves are complicit – for the instant self-gratification of likes, loves and retweets – surrendering deeper values of privacy, intimacy, sincerity, kindness, civility, subtler kinds of knowing, forms of non-self identification and self-doubt. The pandemic has also revealed how social media can so easily be weaponised by neo-fascists and conspiracy theorists whose monstrous cultures of narcissism and cults of personality tap into zeitgeists of fear and misinformation with disastrous political effects.)

5

Yes, it's certainly clear that we adults are experiencing as much difficulty coping as young people. Nearing home, I see an older neighbour has left out on the nature strip what seems a fairly new TV with a note that reads, 'Please take! In perfect working order! I just can't bear to see or hear any more rubbish!' At home, I myself switch from the nightly program the ABC has dedicated to pandemic coverage called 'The Virus', to SBS Food and see Nigella waxing lyrical about the virtues of Aleppo pepper, whereupon my addled mind wanders to the refugee camps of Idlib province, northwestern Syria. I look around the house which is so messy it looks 'like a bomb has hit it' – except this is not quite correct, is it? Since bombs generally land elsewhere...Meanwhile, the Inner Child has gone AWOL. I recall James Baldwin's remark that '[l]ove does not begin and end the way we seem to think it does. Love is a battle, love is a war; love is a growing up.' I start to clean up.

One evening I attend my Zen meditation group by Zoom. The subject of the dharma café is compassion. We are asked by the teacher to reflect on how our ability to be compassionate and our relationships with others may be being challenged during this time. Frozen behind the screen, I can only think of those unreturned phone calls, whether my voicemails will one day be discovered and played by my mother before the abyss grows wider, before the river of forgetting and oblivion becomes unfordable. *I am supposed to be writing this essay, ostensibly on technology*, but I am glad to be silent, for the inner chatter to settle, to cease at least for a little while; to listen and tune in to how others are faring with similar and also radically different conundrums. I wonder can anyone speak, except in a broken-hearted way, to this suffering which is epic because of its scale, its disproportion and whose only known antidote – separation – causes immense kinds of suffering too?

Some are speaking of the #KarunaVirus and calling it Kali Yuga. I don't know about that but I do know Dōgen wrote:

That the self advances and confirms the ten thousand things
is called delusion;
That the ten thousand things advance and confirm the self
is called enlightenment.

I'm not much of a bodhisattva, though, for self does not remain still for long enough; holding on for dear life, self does not entirely drop away. When I sit, traces and contours of the ten thousand things continue endlessly in some existential feedback loop in the mind, and I'm hyperaware of the karmic chain-links of cause, effect and conditioning – what in Mahayana Buddhism is called 'interdependent co-arising' *(Pratītyasamutpāda)*. Looking within, I can't help but see ontologically, as much as with reference to any 'intellectual' or scientific analysis, that we are *already* connected and that our connection and interbeing is inescapable. That, although we ourselves may have created the environmental conditions for the viral mutations of a single pangolin, the pandemic is really only a symptom whose effects we decry because they are now being experienced by our own species; we think ourselves exceptional, quite forgetting that we too are part of the planet's lifeforms and intricately interwoven ecosystems – including its conditions of extinction.

I speak in a broken-hearted way, not only of the ten thousand things but the nearly 11.46 million hectares of habitat and three billion creatures – mammals, reptiles, birds and frogs in the path of the Australian fires – and the continued burning of the one, true Amazon. Caught in an earlier 'storm of progress', Walter Benjamin wrote that '[t]he tradition of the oppressed teaches us that the "state of emergency" in which we live is not the exception but the rule'. Describing the phenomena of this pandemic means acknowledging that what we are seeing is hardly unprecedented or surprising. The virus has simply exposed and intensified gross disparities of wealth and power whose origins, variously in colonialism, slavery and the post-Industrial Age, are in fact the preconditions of our own age of liquid modernity, when the reach of late capitalism through technology and human mastery of the environment (and even designs on neighbouring planets in our galaxy) – that is to say, our agency as humans – has never been greater. This is our kind of catastrophe and ours alone to remedy.

6

I am supposed to be writing this essay on technology, but it's only in the last few weeks I've begun to feel better, to begin to feel more like 'Suneeta'. I'm testing my energy levels. Some days I do very little, finding it enough of a feat just to cook a small meal, eat it, wash dishes, shower and sleep; to be aware of this body-mind, inside/outside, its extraordinary proprioception and capacity to mediate the world beyond. I walk round the block to the community garden and, on days when feeling more heroic, to the village shops and back. I take my opioids and medicines. The mind-fog, an after-effect of anaesthesia, perhaps protects from too much recall and also gives me no choice but to slow down, to observe the small things unfolding, evolving and changing, even dying: the seed

I planted emerging into tufts of mustard greens; the curtain I've made out of an offcut of yellow silk organza to cheer myself billowing out of the bedroom window and getting laddered and wet in the late spring showers, which are said to herald the return of La Niña.

There is still a bit of strain when I exert myself, but this breath is literally the measure of my existence, oxygenating the blood which my heart reliably pumps. It will not do so indefinitely; one day my heart will stop, so the reliability is just an illusion. I tend the wound, a long vertical cut, for which the surgeon when he first saw me afterward apologised. I felt apologetic too, but did not say, for not shaving my legs or privates. After all, the only scissors they gave were tiny, good enough for a child, with sky blue plastic handles in a sterilised packet. It was a difficult surgery, almost one of the most difficult, he told me, as everything was so stuck together...I did not ask him whether he found any pathology with regard to frontal lobe damage, bruxism or irony poisoning. I did not ask if he found ten thousand bits and pieces of plastic inside me. In fragments and not all at once, the details do come back to me. How, at my worst, when every few days I had to be hooked up to someone else's blood, I'd observe, *That's just how connected we are...*

I watch mindless amounts of the SBS Food channel, trying to forget above all the hospital menu which I had come to know by heart, and the dread I felt upon seeing the faces of the orderlies as they drew back the curtain to ask, 'Would you like to do your menu?' I hardly ate and what little I did was often regurgitated. Now I eat whatever I like while watching David Attenborough's *Extinction* on iView and the special livestreaming of the spawning of the Great Barrier Reef. And though I've been told it's probably overkill, I wear the compression stockings. I wear the stockings *out of an abundance of caution*, defiantly, like some Pippi Longstocking of the Covid-19 era, but also with some affection and even loving kindness towards the person I was in the weeks and months gone by. When they caught me handwashing and hanging them from the IV poles at the end of my bed, the nurses would offer me new packets. I found it wasteful they'd put the used ones in landfill every day, but now I stretch my sheathed if hairy legs out on the sofa, imagining my secret stash and the ten thousand places I may go when I can walk about easily again.

The limbic terror is turning into something resembling relief and gratitude for simply being alive. Of course I am aware it could have been a worse scenario, including being in Melbourne, or anywhere else in the world; with exactly the same presentation or something even more dire; without universal healthcare; without friends who, despite their own fears and difficulties, cared enough to visit; to collect things from my home and bring me treats and supplies; to entertain me with books and pamper me with gifts, flowers and phone calls; to check for mail and water my garden; to hear me when I told them I'd rather die than endure the pain any longer. For the women I met, the one who contracted sepsis; the woman who had been diagnosed with stomach cancer; the one I lay next to when I came out of the Covid-19 iso ward who had just had her leg amputated: for these brave soldiers I was quite happy to search for Lang Lang playing Chopin's 'Grande Polonaise Brillante in E-flat Major' on YouTube and even put The Beatles' 'Sgt. Pepper's Lonely Hearts Club Band' on the playlist.

I am supposed to be writing this essay on technology, but before I come to that, I'm Googling a recipe that makes the best hummus;

better than all my efforts so far, it comes out so smooth and doesn't require the forethought of soaked chickpeas, just a pinch of bicarb soda. I crack open one of the ten thousand cans from the war-arsenal. It's 'like eating a cloud' my poet friend affirms when she comes to see me and I try it out on her. We're eager to catch up and yet it's difficult to know where to begin, to find again the place where we left off, since so much has happened and there are ten thousand and more stories to tell... As she balances the plates and I carry the glasses, she reminds me to take it easy and not lift things. She's sorry she couldn't be more there for me. I don't mind, I say, grateful for her kindness and presence here with me right now, aware she has had her share of heartache and upheaval. We sit out the back in the shade of the paperbark which has just begun to shed its ten thousand and more white blossoms, and the rainbow lorikeets screech as we start.

Works Cited

James Baldwin, *The Fire Next Time*, Penguin Books Ltd, London, United Kingdom, 1997.

Walter Benjamin, *Illuminations* (Hannah Arendt, ed.; Harry Zohn trans.), Jonathan Cape Ltd, Great Britain, 1970.

April Bernard, 'Haunt', *New York Review of Books*, 2 July, 2020.

Eihei Dōgen, *Moon in a Dewdrop: Writings of Zen Master Dōgen* (Kazuaki Tanahashi trans.), North Point Press, New York, 1985.

Ali Cobby Eckermann, 'Dip', *Inside My Mother*, The Giramondo Publishing Company, Artarmon NSW, Australia, 2015.

Emmanuel Levinas, *Totality and Infinity* (Alphonso Lingis, trans.), Duquesne University Press, Pittsburgh, PA, 1969.

Ling Ma, *Severance*, Farrar, Straus and Giroux, New York, USA, 2018.

Marianne Moore, 'The Pangolin', *New Collected Poems of Marianne Moore* (Heather Cass White, ed.), Faber & Faber, London UK, 2017.

Arundhati Roy, 'The Pandemic is a Portal', *Financial Times*, 4 April 2020.

William Shakespeare, *Measure for Measure* (The Arden Shakespeare, 3rd Series; A.R. Braunmuller and Robert N. Watson, eds.), Bloomsbury, 2020.

Stevie Smith, *Over the Frontier*, Jonathan Cape Ltd, Great Britain, 1938.

Lao Tse, *Tao Teh Ching: The Way and Its Nature* (John R. Leebrick trans.), Sufi George Books, 2008.

Adam Zagajewski, 'Praise the Mutilated World', *Without End: New and Selected Poems* (Clare Cavanagh, Renata Gorczynski, Benjamin Ivry and C.K. Williams, trans.), Farrar, Straus and Giroux, New York, USA, 2003.

Author Biographies

SUNIL BADAMI is a writer, academic & consultant. His work has been published in nearly every Australian media outlet and literary journal, as well as appearing in *Best Australian Stories* and *Essays*. He devised and presented the national ABC Radio show *Sunday Takeaway*, and has appeared regularly on ABC Radio, Radio National, Double J and ABC TV. He lives in Sydney.

VANESSA BERRY is a writer who works with memory, history, archives and objects. She is the author of four books, including *Gentle and Fierce* (Giramondo, 2021), a memoir about human and animal relationships, and the award-winning *Mirror Sydney* (Giramondo, 2017), about urban environments and change. She is the author of the autobiographical zine series *I Am a Camera* and her zine and illustration works have been exhibited at major Australian galleries. She is a Lecturer in Creative Writing at the University of Sydney.

MIRO BILBROUGH is a Sydney-based writer and filmmaker. Her memoir *In the Time of the Manaroans* (VUP and Ultimo Press) was reviewed as 'the best book of non-fiction published in New Zealand in 2020', and was shortlisted for the Douglas Stewart Prize for Non-fiction, NSW Premier's Literary Awards 2021. She has published poetry widely, including in her chapbook *Small Time Spectre* (Kilmog Press, 2010). Award-winning feature films she has written and directed are *Being Venice* (2012) and *Floodhouse* (2004).

LUKE CARMAN's debut work of fiction, *An Elegant Young Man*, won the 2014 NSW Premier's New Writing Award and was shortlisted for the ALS Gold Medal, the Steele Rudd Short Story Prize and the Readings New Writing Award. His essay collection, *Intimate Antipathies*, was published in June 2019. His second collection of stories, *An Ordinary Ecstasy*, will be published in July 2022.

LAUREN CARROLL HARRIS is a writer and curator.

MADDEE CLARK is a Yugambeh writer and editor living in Narrm on unceded country of the Boonwurrung and Wurundjeri Peoples. He has been published in *Overland*, *The Lifted Brow*, ABC, SBS, and *The Saturday Paper*. He has jointly edited issues of *Liminal Magazine*, *Un Magazine*, and *Archer*.

JUSTIN CLEMENS: Writer of moribund forms. Associate Professor at the University of Melbourne.

LISA FULLER is a Wuilli Wuilli woman from south-east Queensland, who has lived on Ngunnawal and Ngambri Country (Canberra) since 2006. She is doing her PhD in Creative Writing at the University of Canberra. Lisa is an award-winning writer, sessional academic and freelance writer/editor. Her debut novel, *Ghost Bird*, has won awards including the 2020 ACT Book of the Year and the 2020 Queensland Literary Awards Griffith University Young Adult Book Award. Lisa is owned by an insane staffy, lives in a renovation with a patient partner, and battles her inner critic every day.

ELENA GOMEZ lives in Melbourne. She is the author of *Admit the Joyous Passion of Revolt*, *Body of Work*, and several chapbooks and pamphlets.

EDA GUNAYDIN is a Turkish-Australian writer and researcher, whose work explores diaspora, intergenerational trauma and class. Her debut essay collection *Root and Branch* will be released in May 2022 with NewSouth Publishing. You can find her work in *Meanjin*, the *Sydney Review of Books* and others.

TOM LEE is an academic and writer who works in the School of Design at the University of Technology Sydney. He researches the relationship between narrative and technology. Tom's first novel, *Coach Fitz*, was published by Giramondo. His second novel, *Object Coach*, is due out with Upswell in 2022.

JAMES LEY is Contributing Editor with the *Sydney Review of Books*. He is the author of *The Critic in the Modern World: Public Criticism from Samuel Johnson to James Wood* (2014) and co-editor, with Catriona Menzies-Pike, of *The Australian Face: Essays from the Sydney Review of Books* (2017).

FIONA KELLY MCGREGOR has published seven books, most recently the essay collection *Buried Not Dead*, which features in-depth artist profiles and critiques, memoir and urban histories, and was shortlisted for the Victorian Premier's Literary Awards. Her novel *Indelible Ink* won the *Age* Book of the Year. Other books include photoessay *A Novel Idea*, travel memoir *Strange Museums*, short story collection *Suck My Toes/Dirt*, which won the Steele Rudd Award, and the underground classic *chemical palace*. In 2021, Fiona was writer-in-residence at Carriageworks for performance. She is current writer-in-residence at BR Whiting Studio in Rome. In September 2022 Picador will publish the first in a duet of novels based on the life of 1930s petty criminal Iris Webber.

CATRIONA MENZIES-PIKE is the editor of the *Sydney Review of Books*.

OLIVER MOL is the author of *Train Lord* (Penguin Michael Joseph, 2022) and *Lion Attack!* (Scribe, 2015). He is 2020–22 Marten Bequest Scholar for Prose. He is currently living in Georgia.

SUNEETA PERES DA COSTA is based in Sydney on Gadigal land. She writes fiction, non-fiction, plays and poetry. Her latest book, *Saudade* (Giramondo, 2018; Transit, 2019), was shortlisted for the 2019 Australian Prime Minister's Literary Awards, the 2020 Adelaide Festival Awards for Literature, and a finalist in Field Notes' 2020 Tournament of Books. Her literary honours include a Fulbright Scholarship, Australia Council for the Arts BR Whiting Residency, Rome, and an Asialink Arts Creative Exchange to North India.

ELLENA SAVAGE is an author and educator. Her debut essay collection *Blueberries* (2020) was longlisted for the Stella Prize and shortlisted for the VPLA.

MCKENZIE WARK was born in Newcastle NSW but has lived in New York City for many years. She is the author, among other things, of *Reverse Cowgirl* (Semiotexte) and *Philosophy for Spiders* (Duke University Press). Her correspondence with Kathy Acker was published as *I'm Very Into You* (Semiotexte).

LAURA ELIZABETH WOOLLETT is the author of a short story collection, *The Love of a Bad Man* (Scribe, 2016), and two novels, *Beautiful Revolutionary* (Scribe, 2018) and *The Newcomer* (Scribe, 2021). *The Love of a Bad Man* was shortlisted for the Victorian Premier's Literary Award for Fiction and the Ned Kelly Award for Best First Fiction. *Beautiful Revolutionary* was shortlisted for the 2019 Prime Minister's Literary Award for Fiction and the Australian Literature Society Gold Medal. Laura was the City of Melbourne's 2020 Boyd Garret writer-in-residence and is a 2020–22 Marten Bequest scholar for prose.

FIONA WRIGHT is a writer, editor and critic. Her book of essays *Small Acts of Disappearance* won the 2016 Kibble Award and the Queensland Literary Award for non-fiction. Her most recent book is *The World Was Whole*.

Acknowledgements

Sydney Review of Books is an initiative of the Writing and Society Research Centre at Western Sydney University. We were able to commission the essays that appear in this anthology thanks to funding from Create NSW, the City of Sydney, the Australia Council, Creative Victoria and Arts Queensland. Thanks to Andrew Brooks and Alice Desmond for their editorial acumen; to Nick Tapper, Aleesha Paz and Ivor Indyk at Giramondo Books; to Suzanne Gapps and Kate Fagan at the Writing and Society Research Centre.

The essays in this anthology were written on the Country of the Gadigal, Dharawal, Wangal, Wurundjeri, Ngunnawal, Ngambri, Wiradjuri Woiwurrung, Lenape, Wurundjeri, Yuin, Wodi Wodi and Darkinjung peoples. We acknowledge the Traditional Owners of these lands and offer our respects to Elders past, present and emerging. Sovereignty was never ceded and the struggles for justice are ongoing.